UNITY *Without* Compromise

UNITY *Without* Compromise

A Biblical Basis for Christian Union

Steve LaTulippe, MD

XULON ELITE

Xulon Press Elite
2301 Lucien Way #415
Maitland, FL 32751
407.339.4217
www.xulonpress.com

ISBN-13: 978-1-6305-0147-1

To my ever-loving wife who has so graciously and wholeheartedly supported my endeavors in declaring the message of this book.

Table of Contents

Preface

We are living at a crucial time of decision in America and around the globe. The forces opposing Christians and biblical standards, even in our so-called Christian nation, are armed for battle. What was once considered good and noble and acceptable by a Christian standard are now subject to mockery and threats. In the past, God's people had a healthy understanding of doctrine, which enabled them to withstand these attacks and persecutions. Unfortunately, today biblical illiteracy is at an all-time high in our nation, and this problem is compounded by an anything-goes mentality which has even infiltrated the church. Secularists now have a stranglehold on the church, and the time is at hand for returning to the Bible and uniting all Christians as one-church body standing for the true and eternal principles set forth by God.

This book is written to help bring this to pass. By challenging the grievous status quo and exposing some of the most popular and powerful misconceptions that have weakened and divided the universal church to the point of stupor, a call is made to revisit Scripture with clear eyes, so we might see the path before us to real Christian unity based on universal and sound biblical teaching. All Bible quotations are taken from the New King James version.

I am indebted to past theological professors and fellow Christians whose zeal for accurate Bible discernment has influenced me in no small way. I extend the utmost gratitude to Dale

Cornett, former professor at Boise Bible College, whose expertise and invaluable critique and editing have greatly refined my undertaking. I also thank my wife Teresa whose loving support and patience has made the writing of this book possible. I wish also to thank Jack Minor for his professional editing assistance and insightful suggestions and commentary to strengthen this book. The staff at Xulon Press were a delight to work with, and I am most appreciative of their help in bringing this work to fruition. My respect and admiration for all those, past and present, who have paid a price for the cause of real Christianity, no matter the cost, is boundless. May we all join their ranks as we let our light shine in the midst of a very dark world.

Chapter 1

Introduction to the Unity Dilemma

A Body of Christ Divided

Christianity is plagued with a fashionable curse as never before—division. The body of Christ has become so partitioned that nobody can grasp what it actually means to say, "I am a Christian." Conducting research for this book was both daunting and enlightening. I was surprised at how much has been written about the ecumenical movement and other subjects regarding congregational blending and unity. In some cases, attempts have been made to propose solidarity among Roman Catholics and Protestants; and most recently even among Christians, Muslims and other world religions.

This type of oneness was suggested by Ernest FaLardeau who cites many profound and pertinent verses of Scripture in his reflections on Christian unity, blending them with traditions of the Roman Catholic Church.[1] Others have sought for a more stringent and plausible unification such as Barry Callen and James North, who sought a union between two closely affiliated church bodies

(Christian Church/Churches of Christ and the Church of God (Anderson)) that harbor only subtle differences in their church traditions.[2] The authors made many claims of progress toward a unified church, and put forth many new suggestions to promote unity.

Albert Outler, a professor of theology at Southern Methodist University who published his Richard Lectures at the University of Virginia in 1955, opened his first chapter by claiming, "The ecumenical movement is *the* (italics his) great representative occurrence in modern Christian history." He further asserted, "Within living memory, it has wrought a revolution—in the temper and spirit in which Christians regard one another, in the climate of theological work and church life, in the hopes of reversing the centuries-old drift into division, in the prospect of overcoming the stubborn, self-righteous fragmentation of the people of God."[3] He proposed that the conduit of ecumenical success derives from a de-emphasis of the *sola Scriptura* tenet of the Protestant Reformation, favoring our common historical Christian roots as the foundation for community over all doctrinal issues.

Several years later, the unity challenge was discoursed by a more conservative Reformed theologian, D. Martin Lloyd-Jones, who acknowledged, "No question is receiving so much attention at the present time in all branches and divisions of the Christian church as the question of church unity."[4]

In his book, *The Basis of Christian Unity*, Lloyd-Jones dissects the two key Scripture passages most often quoted in appealing to Christian unity. He opens with a token lament to the disparity within the church community, assenting that we must all regard schism as a grievous sin. After addressing the complexity of the problem, he seems to undermine his unity quest by declaring that unity "must never be thought of, therefore, as something voluntary." Rather he asserts, "It is something which is inevitable because it is the result of being born into a given family."[5] Here he renders an interesting interpretation of John 17, but his claim seems illogical. If unity is inevitable, then why did Jesus pray for it?

In a subsequent chapter, Lloyd-Jones appears to contradict his first assertion of an involuntary default to unity by saying, "there is no unity unless we are agreed in these things and participating in them."[6] Agreeing and participating are voluntary acts. These sorts of problems normally arise because of the logical and understandable tension between our desire to be one in Christ and our equally fervent desire to not compromise what we regard as essential doctrines. As Christians, we all recognize the importance of a unified body, but we should rightly refuse to accept unity at any price. The ultimate question is, where do we draw the line? How much are we willing to compromise our convictions before considering someone as not being *in Christ*?

In some form or other the battle for oneness among church groups has raged for decades, but the battlefield is small. Few Christians caught up in the daily bustle of life have the time or energy to fight over unity, as seems to occur between Christian scholars. Most Christians feel they can live comfortably and happily with division. To them, it's not a big issue. In fact, it's more pleasant and comfortable this way. You go to your church; I'll go to mine. No judgments are insinuated and none are taken. But this attitude still leaves us in a predicament.

This was not God's plan for His church. Despite all efforts to bridge the unity gaps, the number of denominations in America is growing, not shrinking. The 12th Edition of Mead's Handbook of Denominations in The United States lists 232 "religious groups" in America.[7] (And this is not the latest edition.) This list includes seven sects of Judaism, numerous Christian denominations, and a smattering of Islamic and other offbeat religions. Division throughout history seems the norm rather than the exception. Nonetheless, we must applaud the efforts of our unity crusaders, however delusional or impotent we may perceive their efforts. The battle for unity is a worthy cause. I was delighted by reading of such fervor among the various denominational scribes who recognized the urgency and necessity for a unified body of Christ. Their yearning is heartfelt, and their quest is noble.

Unity of Purpose versus Doctrine

In some isolated circumstances, unity has prevailed. Examples include various medical missions trips attended by an assortment of Christians from diverse backgrounds. They unify for the common good, to bring healing and encouragement to those suffering from physical ailments. This unity in a common goal is a profound statement of Christ's love. These people are doers of the word. In these rare circumstances, however, we behold a unity of purpose, not a unity of doctrine.

Regardless, what we do observe is the beauty of a body of medical personnel acting as one, putting aside lesser differences of doctrine for a unified and good purpose. How splendid a testimony this is to those benefiting from such comradeship. Imagine how much more powerful we could be as a force for good—truly a force for God—if such spiritual unity became the norm. Most certainly this is precisely what Jesus envisioned as He prayed to His Father that we might be one. The benefits of *unus corpus* Christianity are obvious to all. The desire for oneness is present as a subtle ingredient in the stew of every sincere believer's faith. Just as the earnestly pondering mind intuitively senses the Divine Presence in the magnificent design of the universe, so the ardent disciple of Jesus longs for the very oneness God intended for His universal Church. But despite all the literature written on the subject of church unity, I frankly see little true impetus behind the oneness movement. If it isn't happening locally where we live, then it isn't happening abroad.

The Unity Spectrum

An important distinction must be made between ecumenism, denominationalism, and the Christian oneness described in the biblical church model. The ecumenical movement is essentially an effort to destroy barriers between denominations by appealing to our common roots in the Abrahamic tradition, thereby reducing the terms of Christian brotherhood to its least common denominator.

This goal does have some merit and appeal, as the ecumenist seeks to promote acceptance and understanding of each other's different traditions in the hope of engendering cooperation among the denominations. The problem with this approach is that this sense of commonality can only go so far. The basic message is: Let's hold hands and accept one another despite our differences. The more extreme ecumenists even suggest that whatever our differences, they aren't nearly as important as working side by side to reform society, to show the world that Christians care. But expecting a unification of religious groups based on core religious beliefs is quite a different matter. For most Christians, to transgress denominational boundaries is to betray their loyalties, indeed, to compromise their faith. Ask yourself, how inclusive would *you* be in defining the criteria of Christian fellowship?

The Growing Divide

Many of our present-day Christian denominations have existed for hundreds of years. Over time, many different forms of worship have evolved, these being now so varied in construct as to intimidate or confuse the unfamiliar brother. I suspect the majority of Christians would oppose a unified church not so much on doctrinal grounds but on a passionate desire for the sweet familiarity of what they have grown accustomed to in their worship services. As I write, many small churches in America are closing their doors simply because they refuse to rid themselves of the organ and hymnals they associate with true Christianity. Yes, better to fold and die than permit any change of tradition that might accommodate new converts to Christ. Traditional bulwarks supersede all quests to reach the lost and nurture real spiritual growth. Nothing so plainly exposes a shallow spirituality, if such a thing can even be considered spiritual. We might call this the antithesis of ecumenism.

While the principles of denominationalism may overlap ecumenical ideology, the former, by its nature, is at odds with ecumenism. Some of the distinctions among various Christian religious sects are so pronounced that a neutral observer might suspect they were each birthed from a different source rather than from a single composite work such as the Bible. Although the pulpit messages may have many common points, the points of distinction are what matter most to the denominationalist, for they are what defines the denomination, and this pride of affiliation sustains the details of distinction from other bodies of Christ.

For this reason, a Methodist preacher could not be asked to fill in for a Lutheran minister for fear he might offend some in the congregation simply because a Methodist is not trained to be a Lutheran. Likewise, a Baptist would feel sorely out of place attending a Pentecostal worship service "because, you know, things just aren't done that way in our church," a member would say. The Pentecostal member would likely feel stifled and downright bored in a conservative Baptist assembly for lack of entertainment value. Such thoughts are not likely to be openly spoken, but each sect understands and respects his *a priori* loyalty to his denominational beliefs and practices.

The tacit message of ecumenicalism is understood: I'm okay. You're okay. So let's be nice to each other. Although this mindset is certainly a step up from denominations bitterly criticizing each other over petty details and competing for members as though church membership were a sort of religious commodity, both ideologies are still a far cry from our Lord's supplication before His sacrificial death. This clearly is not what Jesus had in mind when he prayed for the unity of all His followers. What then *did* He have in mind? This is the question that must be answered. Once understood, we are obligated as Christians to act according to His will, not ours. The answer can only be found in the words of Scripture. If a biblical pattern of worship and community can be elucidated and practiced, then unity is sure to follow.

What is vividly obvious in most books on unification is each author using the topic of Christian unity as a platform to propound his own denominational slant on the subject. That shall never do, for it can only further divide. By the end of my investigational reading, I was frankly weary of all the pitches for "unity on my terms." Can the lack of progress toward a unified church be further explained? Can any real progress toward Christian unity be made? Surely it can. God never commands us to do something without giving us the ability to do it.

Jesus relates His desire that all men be saved (1 Tim. 2:4) while also asserting that "narrow is the gate and difficult is the way which leads to life, and there are few who find it" (Matt. 7:14). Jesus desires that all Christians be one in mind and body, but the way to unity seems more difficult than entering the narrow gate. Certainly unity is at least a theoretical possibility if Jesus Himself prayed for it.

This is my sole reason for writing this book: to elucidate how, on God's own terms, oneness is achievable without compromising Bible truths. Given the aforementioned limitations of Christian scholarship due to the prismatic distortions of scholarly biases— yes, even scholars are full of human flaws—this book is written with a global perspective on church cohesiveness based on the fundamental model set forth by God Himself. I appeal to both scholars and newborn Christians with frankness and in a spirit of humility (since I too have biases) to rethink their own theologies.

The book is explicitly written with no polemic intent, but it necessarily deals with some hard and emotionally-charged topics that divide us. The book is not intended to induce feelings of guilt, ire, or offense. Rather it is a call for candid sincerity among all who profess Jesus as their Savior to question their own beliefs and traditions in light of Scripture, and to allow God's Spirit of unity to have His way among us. This work is also a plea to reject all manmade notions of what may superficially appear to be biblical in origin but is not. The reader is challenged to supplant all divisive half-truths and weak dogmas with a fuller meaning of God's Word, without compromise, and with a genuine heart and mind to pursue a unified body in Christ. Toward this end, my focus is to openly explore some major issues that divide us, and demonstrate how a diligent and honest search of the Scriptures may clear the fog and topple the walls that unnecessarily divide us.

Achieving Christian Unity

Many excellent works have been written on the science of Bible interpretation, called hermeneutics, and much is to be gained from reading and studying such quality textbooks. (A few good sources are listed in the bibliography.) I do not seek to replicate such manuals but rather to highlight the basic essentials of sound interpretation, to expose the ways in which most Christians tend to violate or ignore these rules of interpretation, and to elucidate the root cause of the major obstacles to achieving a unified Christian body. Finally, in the spirit of true Christian fellowship, I appeal to the hearts of all brothers and sisters in Christ to contend for *the faith* (Jude 3), not for my faith or your faith, but for the one true faith as loyal and steadfast ambassadors for Christ, knowing that the consequences of our battle for unity are profound. The outcome of this spiritual warfare will influence the eternal fate of many, including our own offspring. But the holy quest for unity itself shall yield much good fruit in every true soldier of God. When our ephemeral earthly life has ended, think of the blessings we shall receive if we have sincerely and humbly strived to actually be an answer to our Savior's own final earthly prayer.

Endnotes

[1] Ernest FaLardeau, *That All May Be One: Catholic Reflections on Christian Unity*, Paulist Press, New York, 2000.

[2] Barry Callen and James North, *Coming Together in Christ*, College Press, Joplin, 1997.

[3] Albert C. Outler, *The Christian Tradition and the Unity We Seek*, Oxford University Press, New York, 1957, Chapter 1, "The Ecumenical Fact," p. 3.

[4] D. Martin Lloyd-Jones, *The Basis of Christian Unity*," The Banner of Truth Trust, Carlisle, 2003, p. 1.

[5] Ibid., p.13.

[6] Ibid., p. 37.

[7] Frank S. Mead, et al., *Handbook of Denominations in the United States*, 12th ed., Abingdon Press, Nashville, 2005.

Chapter 2

Is Unity Even Possible?

An Unforeseen Dilemma

Years ago, serving as chaplain of the 1993 freshman medical school class at Loma Linda University, I was asked to lead a Bible study. Those assembled for the first meeting represented a potpourri of Christians from various backgrounds, each with their own nuances of beliefs that could potentially be a source of conflict in the course of our study. Having experienced in my recent past a rather brief but turbulent pulpit ministry, I quickly recognized the situation for what it was: a brewing disaster from the start.

Loma Linda is regarded by some as the "Mecca" of the Seventh-day Adventist Church, and as chaplain for the Class of '97 Loma Linda University School of Medicine, I felt a responsibility to respect their traditional beliefs without compromising my own integrity. Present in the room at our first meeting were Adventists, Baptists, Lutherans, a Roman Catholic, Pentecostals, and a few from other denominations. How could we possibly have a Bible study? And then I was struck by the utter folly of my trepidation. This was a *Bible study*, wasn't it? And by definition we were here to study the Bible. What's so hard about that?

To Study and Not Offend?

God exhorts His followers to diligently study His Word, and study we shall, I vowed. Pondering potential topics for our study caused me more consternation, however. Should we discuss an isolated topic, a scriptural passage, or just work through a specific book of the Bible? Realizing the opportunity before me for strengthening or for weakening, for building walls or building bridges, I contemplated a good number of passages of Scripture that would most certainly lead to conflict if certain subjects were broached. I could either commit the odious crime of ecumenical complicity by avoiding every possible topic of conflict, or I could establish a few ground rules.

Choosing the latter, I established the first dictum of this Bible study: *No opinions shall be given* by me or anyone else. After establishing a few other simple rules of law and order in the interest of maintaining unity in the group, what ensued was a most intriguing exploration of the jewels of God's instruction manual as ever I have experienced. We became a cohesive and united little body of Christ, a local church body who blended itself into a biblical organism of oneness. In a very real and practical sense, albeit on a small scale, we were an affirmative answer to the real Lord's prayer in John 17, as Jesus prayed on His way to Gethsemane.

Imagine... A Global Christian Church

From this study I tasted the refreshing waters of Christian unity that derives from a group of disciples setting themselves on the path to knowing God by doing justice to His word. Ever since that time, I have yearned for a similar union among all Christians, just as Jesus must have yearned as He prayed to His Father before departing this world to again join Him in the heavenly realm.

Imagine, in any town where you might live, Christians meeting to hear the word of God proclaimed, where all present are encouraged to abide in God's word and to follow closely in His steps, without any distortions of God's truth. How refreshing it would be to travel to wherever Christians were gathering and feel right at home. Imagine freedom from all manmade religious trappings. No fear of unknown denominational protocols. Just read some Scripture, encourage and support one another, do some praying, break bread in remembrance of Jesus, and allow God's Spirit to work in us as we mutually submit to His will. Shouldn't this be the desire of every person devoted to God? Think of what blessings might shower upon us if this sort of unified assembly occurred weekly across the globe. What power of conviction, what attestation to the world that our God is One God, and the Body of Christ is one unified assembly of like-minded people, of like faith—the people of God. Nothing more, nothing less. This unity would catch the world's attention. That's what Jesus wanted.

Which Is the Right Church?

Well-known Christian counselor and founder of New Way Ministries Larry Crabb painfully verbalized his yearning for such a church in his book, *Real Church*, where he laments the pitiable state of contemporary churches in America. His heartfelt contention that something is wrong, something is missing in our churches, drew some sharp criticism from church leaders. But the truth always hurts. He is square on the mark when he exposes the crisis of denominationalism by asking a simple but convicting question. "What church do I want to go to? Conservative? Liberal? Evangelical? Mainline? Big? Small? Liturgical? Charismatic? Reformed? Seeker-sensitive? Emergent?"[1]

Every sincere Christian who has a solid grasp on Scripture must harbor this inner struggle borne out of a divided church. A seasoned

Christian cannot attend a church service of one denomination and fully participate in its worship without feeling some degree of hypocrisy or guilt because to affirm one church is to negate another. Every new Christian who joins a local church believes they have joined the greatest organized unit in the world—the one, true body of Christ. They assume fellowship with the right church, unaware of the many schisms in Christ's body.

The Crumbling Unified Church

But look around you. Such is not the case. Instead, every church raises its banner of "truth" based on its own set of rules. The criticism Larry Crabb received is understandable (though unwarranted), because he committed the "unpardonable sin" of stripping back the veneer, exposing the real impetus of every denomination. Crabb unveils the curse of all denominations as "the mission of getting people into organized religion, of persuading secular people to sign up in support of institutionalized Christianity that is more a power-hungry corporation than a loving community, of joining people to a culture that isolates itself from the world around it to preserve its proud illusion of humility and holiness, and of buying into a religious system that cares more about rules than relationships, likes management and fears mystery, and values successful organization over reviving communities."[2]

This schizophrenic bride is *not* what the Bridegroom envisioned. What we have in most churches today is a new brand of Pharisees and Sadducees, the blind leading the blind, each unwilling to envision the church as Jesus intended it to be. This is a sad testimony to the power of Satan working among us. Certainly, the search for a perfect church is futile, but can a church be found that humbly and lovingly submits to the full truth of Scripture, rightly interpreted and fleshed out in holy living, without any mask of pretentiousness?

Three Reasons for Failed Oneness

Truth be told, total harmony and unity of the universal, visible Christian Church will never be attained for at least three reasons. First and foremost, *we are taught this in Scripture.* Jesus recognized at the inception of his earthly ministry that His radical message of salvation would bring division in the world, and He makes this point very clear when He asks, "Do you suppose that I came to give peace on earth?" Then, leaving no room for doubt, He immediately responds: "I tell you, not at all, but rather division" (Luke 12:51). The obvious wedge is between those who accept and those who reject His words. If the message of the cross "is foolishness to those who are perishing" (1 Cor. 1:18), then obviously it will never be universally accepted. The unrepentant of heart shall in no way receive the message of salvation, nor partake of the kingdom of God.

But Jesus later warns that division would also emanate from within the church body itself. Remember the words He spoke to the multitudes that likely included not a few impious leaders of their time, warning them, "Not everyone who says to me, 'Lord, Lord,' shall enter the kingdom of heaven" (Matt. 7:21). Even in the first-century church, the leaven of faction was already spreading. The apostle Paul attested to this fact when he voiced his observations and protested to the church at Corinth, "When you come together as a church, I hear that there are divisions among you, and in part I believe it" (1 Cor. 11:18). This division, though disheartening, surely came as no surprise since he previously forewarned the Christian churches he had recently established "that after my departure savage wolves will come in among you, not sparing the flock. Also from among yourselves men will rise up, speaking perverse things, to draw away the disciples after themselves" (Acts 20:29-30).

The fact is, evil exists in this world and deceivers abound, even within the church. Since the inception of the church age on that glorious day of Pentecost, imposters have infiltrated the church. Many believers have been led astray to their destruction by the venom of these asps. If the phrase erroneously attributed to P.T. Barnum, "There's a sucker born every minute" is true, then gullible followers of false teachers are in big trouble. While the phrase may exaggerate the ineptitude of mankind, it does accurately reflect the cunning motives of those who would gladly prey on man's fickle and naïve nature, often without a hint of awareness among those being led to the snare.

Deception is often palatable. It may look good, sound good, and feel good, but still betrays the truth. One self-declared unity contender, for example, boldly affirms, "It is not important so much that we believe in God but that God believes in us."[3] Such a statement exposes the author's total disregard for Scripture, as this concept is foreign to what the Bible teaches. This writer's formula for unity delves into a form of nebulous mysticism, exposed by his fallacious appeal, "Just think of the potential for theological discussion if Jesus were the One at work in the conversation. Why not let Jesus himself comment?"[4] Has not Jesus already commented through Scripture? What more commentary do we need? We are made holy and one by God's truth as already declared in the Bible (John 17:17). Such empty appeals to unity for the sake of unity alone have nothing to do with Jesus's prayer for the oneness of his disciples.

The apostle Paul clearly revealed how this threat of false teachings may be subtle and even have the appearance of beauty; but it will also have dire consequences for the Christian brotherhood, and for those who might otherwise be led to the truth. The church suffers immensely from all forms of division and fallacy. Consider the words of the founder of Mormonism, Joseph Smith, who claimed, "I felt some desire to be united with them but so great were the confusion and strife among the different denominations, that it was impossible for a person young as I was, and so unacquainted with men and things, to come to any certain conclusion who was right and who was wrong"[5]

The magnitude of this dilemma is even greater in our present time. Pity the poor person who takes up his Bible one day and is convicted in his heart to follow God. Where does he go? What is the right church? Who will help him along in his spiritual walk? Or who will taint his views, and how, once he has established himself in a local church?

Even when accurately proclaimed, biblical truths are not always tolerated, obeyed, or clearly understood. Those who would reject the teachings of Christianity based on the acts of misbehaving Christians are no less hypocritical than the Christians they renounce. But when Christians themselves reject the message of truth, the question must be asked, are they really Christians? Many a faithful and discerning preacher has been ruthlessly ousted from his local church by wolves shepherding the flock and church members who dislike their own sin being exposed. Some church leaders defiantly choose to reject God's teachings as faithfully proclaimed by the preacher, and the preacher pays the price. Many ecclesiastical officers spurn God's design for the church in favor of their own personal agenda. They seek power, wishing to preserve their manmade traditions. Or they lust after some other unholy cause.

What exudes from such visible churches is a river of florid squalor, polluted with poor doctrine and replete with spiritually impotent disciples. They harbor a total disregard for the richness of God's teaching and for the deepest need of the burdened human soul—the knowledge of salvation through Jesus Christ. A substitute for God's church design, however creative and unique, will always fail. As Lawrence Richards attests, "If we confuse the church with an organization or an institution, and lose sight of it as believers-in-intimate-relationship, we will find no guidelines on which to pattern renewal. But if we keep the scriptural concept in clear focus, the guidelines are many."[6]

The "if" in that last sentence is huge. Keeping Scripture in clear focus is the essential prerequisite for likeness of mind. And for this very reason, unity shall never prevail. The clever enemy always attacks the most vital source first.

A second reason we shall never attain to perfect unity in the church is because *there simply is no cure for willful ignorance*. Cultists capitalize on this principle to ensnare their many victims. Some people, being perhaps overwhelmed by the complexity of life, prefer to be led by the hand and told exactly what they should and should not do. They are willingly oblivious to the source of evil deception before them, satisfied with having a nose ring placed to be led down a spurious path. Just hop on board and follow the tracks, wherever they lead. The unwitting cult-train passengers find the clickety-clack mantra of the railroad tracks comforting and predictable. Though the tracks may terminate in a town called Destruction, they enjoy the comfortable ride and would never consider disembarking the train of doom.

Others, choosing complacent ignorance, are company loyalists who willfully reject God's full instruction in favor of their congregation that has nurtured them since early childhood. Being born into a church, they dare not question its teachings or principles. Blindly accepting the established creed, they see no need to search further in the deep well of divine wisdom. They are fully satisfied to gently row in their calm waters, and they frown on anyone making waves. Feasting on a pie during the after-church socials is more of a delicacy than the Bread of Life, and faithful attendance at all church gatherings culminates in the highest pleasure in their social circle. They "tithe" to support the costs of their clubhouse, cheerfully sacrificing more of their hard-earned money when the roof needs restored or some other pseudo-urgent need arises. Matters of doctrine, inner discipline, and spiritual formation take a back seat to faithfulness to their commodious guild.

Still others, out of spiritual neglect, over-commitment to worldly pursuits, or possibly out of pure laziness, choose the beaten path of blind affirmation. They accept as truth whatever they are told from the pulpit or what they read in Sunday school or small group study handouts. Not that the handouts are necessarily erroneous, but digging deep into Scripture is hard work. To know God intimately is laborious and risky. It costs us something. It takes time. It requires thinking spiritual thoughts. It means hours of hard study. It also demands a response as the sword of the Spirit hearkens the soul. Let's face a hard fact. Responding to God's call to be "a living sacrifice" (Rom 12:1) is something quite foreign to most of us, except for a token hour or two once a week when we shine in our brightest veneer. We smooth over the words *living sacrifice,* placing a great deal of emphasis on the living with very little emphasis on the sacrificing. Living sacrifice? Combining those two words is unsettling in our complacent minds.

Not long ago I attended a Bible study class with a handout excerpting the Good Shepherd passage (John 10). The hour-long study delved into a discussion that yielded a detailed account of all the fine and not-so-fine qualities and characteristics of sheep: the texture of wool, the stupidity of the pea-brained creatures, and all the fine attributes a sheep farmer considers essential to raising such beasts. Trivialities aside, the intent and beauty of the passage was never explored; its meaning was totally obscured by the mundane. Is this disregard for such a profound Scripture lesson not an act of willful ignorance or laziness? All hearers went away satisfied, fulfilled, and self-amused in their spiritual torpor. Willful ignorance is much like smoking cigarettes. It is toxic, insidious, malodorous, and sometimes lethal.

A third and critical impediment to the indivisible church must be disclosed. ***Most essential teachings of Scripture are so***

straightforward that it takes a true scholar to confuse the issue. Perhaps the greatest reason for church disunity occurs because Christians have no solid grasp of even the elementary teachings of Christ. How many professing Christians have even enough Bible knowledge to lead an unbeliever to Christ? Who has rendered the essential doctrines so difficult to understand and communicate? The core teachings of the Bible are so simple to understand that only an educated theologian can muddy the waters of comprehension. Think of the implications. The average minister, small group leader, or Bible-study teacher leans heavily on semi-scholarly commentaries on the Bible, rather than take the time to delve into the word themselves. What doctrines are clouded by the nuances of personal bias and denominational inclinations permeating these commentaries?

Sadly, we have too many scholars and educators among the denominations who eloquently and convincingly elaborate on their "designer brand" of Christianity, forcing the entire Bible to fit their particular truth. This designer theology derives from myopic interpretations of Scripture that lead to doctrinal dogmas that overstate or understate a biblical truth, or aggrandize one biblical teaching to the exclusion of another, sometimes forsaking all reason and conveniently forgetting that the entire Bible needs to be taken in context.

The designer theologian must, above all else, maintain a scrupulous adherence and loyalty to his preconceived central dogmas, and his cardinal biases must frame the whole of his interpretation of every passage of Scripture. So if you pick up a written work, you are never disappointed in finding the Calvinist's focus on "effectual calling" or the Seventh-day Adventist's central dogma of the Sabbath day. To the one, God's sovereignty must forever be defended; to the other, the "right" day of worship is tantamount. Likewise, the Roman Catholic must never neglect the "Holy Mary, Mother of God," and the Quaker must, above all else, reference "the Inner Light." But let's not exclusively pick on these representative denominations. Some emotionally charged biases and tenets are likely proclaimed in one form or another within every existing church in America and globally.

The problem with this decorative scholarship is that every customized theological framework leads to a new denomination. How interesting that each discerning scholar boasts his contrived doctrine with a militant determination to conquer all dissenters and increase his quasi-spiritual territory.

Read any of the books in print on the topic of church unity and you will find delicately fabricated models of institutional presuppositions put forth with such eloquence of denominational bias that the idea of real Christian union is illusory. D. Martin Lloyd-Jones presents some highly insightful views as he writes on the subject of unity. He states, "It is a tragedy that division ever entered into the life of the church. In addition, we must all regard schism as a grievous sin."[7] But he then touts his denominational version of the unity passages, at times so blatantly as to discredit his own thesis.

Still, his intentions are good, and he does make a very good point: unity at all cost leads to an unacceptable compromise of God's word. However, we are still confounded by a very serious dilemma. When scholars from every Christian sect expound their own versions of what the true meaning of oneness in Christ entails, what remains in its scholarly path is a sea of confusion among the pure in heart who simply want to belong to *the* family of God. Ultimately, the crags of division deepen, and unity is rendered even less likely than before each scholar's work has been mentally and spiritually digested. As each author seeks to set the record straight, the heap of theological propaganda burgeons, and discord is congealed among the existing denominations. To the unreached masses, Christians appear to reside in a world of polytheistic monotheism. We claim "one Lord," and we espouse "one faith." But we are divided in our hearts on so many issues that we achieve *anything but* one body and one mind.

A Futile Endeavor?

Human nature being what it is, we can be assured of never realizing an unbroken Christian body this side of glory. So what's the use of going forward? The answer is very simple. Jesus must have had a very good reason for praying to His Father "that they may be one" (John 17:11, 22). If oneness was Jesus's foremost prayer before going to Calvary, then His petition must weigh heavily in its importance to the church—to us. We certainly must be in good standing with the Lord if we pursue unity on *His terms*. And that is the point; not the attainment of unity, but the pursuit of unity shall have its good work in us. When we seek unity, we seek spiritual treasure. Each time we join two hearts in accordance with God's intent, we receive the blessing of knowing we are in harmony with God's will. When Jesus taught his disciples how to pray, He included the words, "Thy will be done" (Matt. 6: 10). He has told us His will.

Endnotes

[1] Larry Crabb, *Real Church*, Thomas Nelson, Nashville, 2009, p. xiv.

[2] Ibid., p. 47.

[3] Callan Slipper, *Five Steps to Living Christian Unity*, New York City Press, Hyde Park, 2013, p. 13.

[4] Ibid., p. 25.

[5] Joseph Smith, *Joseph Smith Tells His Own Story…*, Deseret News, Salt Lake, undated, p. 2.

[6] Lawrence O. Richards, *A New Face for the Church*, Zondervan Publishing House, Grand Rapids, 1970, p. 85.

[7] D Martin Lloyd-Jones, *The Basis of Christian Unity*, Banner of Truth Trust, Edinburg, 2003, p. 1.

Chapter 3

What's at Stake?

Shortly before Jesus was led away to culminate the most consequential act in the history of mankind, His redemptive sacrifice on the cross, the apostle John (Chapter 17) tells us that He "lifted up His eyes to heaven, and said: 'Father, the hour has come. Glorify Your Son, that Your Son also may glorify You'" (v. 1). He then prayed for his disciples. "Sanctify them by Your truth. Your word is truth" (v. 17). And then he prayed "also for those who will believe in Me through their word; that they all may be one, as You, Father, are in Me, and I in You; that they also may be one in Us, that the world may believe that You sent Me" (vv. 20-21).

Doesn't it seem a bit odd that the Savior of the world, as He is nearing the end of His three-year earthly ministry with twelve less-than-sterling students, would pray for unity? Of all that He might have prayed for at His crucial hour, why did He pray for oneness among His followers? If persecution was coming, it seems He should have prayed for their physical and emotional strength. Since His dozen disciples didn't appear at all scholarly, He might have prayed for their diligence in studying all that He taught them. Or Jesus could have prayed for boldness of character to charge ahead and loudly proclaim His message of salvation, which shouldn't have been all that hard to understand. It was a very simple message that even the lowly apostles should have comprehended. But at the time, they still didn't get it. Perhaps Jesus should have asked His Father to sharpen their minds. When the apostle Thomas asked Jesus, "How can we know the way?" Jesus replied very simply, "I am the way, the truth and the life. No one comes to the Father except through Me" (John 14:5-6). The path to oneness with God couldn't have been stated more succinctly. With such a simple and straightforward message, how could Jesus have foreseen any problem of disunity arising?

A Battle for the Bible

The trouble with the message of salvation arises not from any complexity or confusing statements, but from the hearts of men. When Jesus affirmed to His Father, "Your word is truth" (John 17: 17), and then stated that believers would know Jesus through this word or message, He identified the battleground for God's kingdom—His words of truth. These words are compiled in the form of the sacred writings we call the Bible. If the enemy of God ever sought to strike at the most vital source of strength for God's kingdom, he would directly attack the word of God. If this message could be negated, blurred, questioned, challenged, ridiculed or otherwise attacked, then the body of Christ's believers could be easily divided. One does not require an advanced degree in military offensive tactics to strategize an effective plan to conquer and divide the army of God. If the truth of God's word could be undermined, then fractioning God's family would be easy work. Jesus knew that unity among all His followers was the vital force necessary to spreading the word of God throughout the world. Unity is powerful in any form. Unity among Christians unleashes a divine power in the world to overcome all the evil forces known to man.

Have you ever observed such unity among Christians today? Outside of denominational boundaries, the answer is, not likely.

When we look around at the world of Christianity, Jesus's unity prayer seems not at all to have been answered in the affirmative. This raises a host of questions. What was Jesus thinking as He prayed, "that they all may be one"? In today's modern Christian world, doesn't His prayer seem just a little absurd? After all, being God, Jesus had foreknowledge. He knew the church would be divided. Ought we to sorrowfully accept the fact of a divided church, or should His prayer also be our fervent prayer? Is church oneness nothing more than a divine pipe dream? Was He expressing merely an ideal? Was it an act of desperation? Or was Jesus praying for something that might actually exist in the real world? Let's face it. Practically speaking, most Christians, regardless of brand, would consider the unification of the church desirable but totally unrealistic.

Only the most naïve believer would consider real unity achievable. Most local churches struggle to maintain some semblance of unity under their own roofs. On the other hand, any genuine follower of Christ would consider that the real Lord's Prayer (not the model prayer taught to His disciples) epitomizes the importance of Christian unity in the mind of God. It just makes sense. God is One. We are clearly taught by the imprisoned Paul that "There is one body and one Spirit… one Lord, one faith, one baptism; one God and Father of all" (Eph. 4:4-5). We are even told there is "one bread" (1 Cor. 10:17). So if we already have all this oneness, then why did Jesus pray for it? The answer really is not all that elusive, but it does require some understanding of the Bible, which we'll get into later. What's important is that Jesus did pray for the unity of all His followers, for oneness no different from the oneness He enjoys with His Father. This prayer certainly was recorded primarily for our benefit. Jesus prayed for solidarity in His followers because of the goodness and peace that prevails apart from disunion. As the Preacher wrote, "A threefold cord is not quickly broken" (Eccl. 4:12). Oneness in Christ yields more good than we can ever imagine. Try to envision the beautiful force of a one-church system.

The Impact of a United Church

Without analyzing too deeply the meaning of this unity prayer, let's look at some advantages of such unity, and the consequences of disunity. What's at stake? Jesus puts it simply and concisely: "that the world may believe that you sent Me" (John 17:21). There it is! He prays for every Christian convert to live, think, breathe, pray, fellowship, serve and love each other in the same way Jesus and His Father commune in spirit. When the unbelieving world witnesses this kind of unity, others may also believe that Jesus was sent to earth by His Father to spill His redemptive blood for them, too. Thus, the stakes of unity are very high—a matter of spiritual life or death. Inferred in Jesus's prayer is the profound fact that without unity the world may *not* believe.

A blaring testimony to this fact is exemplified in the famous spiritual leader of India, Mahatma Gandhi, who very likely would have converted to Christianity were it not for the arrogance and bitter divisiveness he saw among Christians. Gandhi witnessed firsthand the strife and divisions that plagued the church, how Christians so often mistreated and maligned one another. Imagine the impact for good Gandhi may have wrought for Christianity with his influence among his people, had only Christians sought to render due their affirmation of loyalty and love to all Christians alike. As stated in an old Restoration Movement slogan, "The world will not be *won* until Christians are *one*." Unity is power.

The souls of countless billions weigh in the balance, and among these are our own precious family members and friends. We must realize that the unbelieving world does not differentiate between our various religious sects. The world sees only the actions and hears the words of professing Christians; and how we interact with one another bears heavily on our credibility. The genuine Christian who fosters unity by practicing sincere love for the brotherhood prepares the way for those needing to hear the word of truth. The foundation for Christian unity can only be built on the bulwark of God's truth manifest in His word. By God's design for growing His church, He uses faithful people who have made His priorities their priorities. To the extent that the Christian church prevails, righteousness and goodness will multiply in proportion to that growth. This is what Jesus implies in His prayer.

The history of Christianity reveals that the triumph of good over evil also is at stake. While we may acknowledge the ultimate victory of Christ at His second coming, we shouldn't for a moment ignore the practical daily impact of modern Christianity on our present world. Think of how Christianity has changed the norms and values of countless societies. No other religion has influenced the abolition of slavery, elevated the status of women, or contended for the protection of the innocent and weak, more than the Christian Way. No other object of devout worship in any religion has offered a means of salvation apart from works of human merit. Indeed, the foundation for American democracy was borne out of a professed faith in biblical truth and a determination to live by the Creator's standards. The inherent value of every human being is nowhere more clearly elucidated than in Holy Writ.

Like no other country before us, the "one nation under God" has cast its rays of liberty and hope across the globe. Anyone who has studied the likes of Marx, Mussolini, and Hitler knows the evil core of Socialism, Fascism and Communism. These political systems of godless men led to the widespread oppression and torture of the human body and soul, even unto death. For those who know nothing about living life in light of eternity, and for those not knowing or caring that an all-loving God is watching them, hopelessness abounds. Being estranged from Christ in a godless world means "having no hope" (Eph. 2:12).

A cold, brutal lawlessness prevails in all godless societies, whereby rights are whimsically determined by government rather than from God. Only in a Christian society do we see the esteemed value of the individual, the sanctity of human life, and the equality of all men under God being honored. Indeed, such was the conclusion of the French historian Alexus de Tocqueville who affirmed, "In America it is religion which leads to enlightenment and the observance of divine laws which lead men to liberty."[1] He further attests to the unifying force of Christianity in facilitating and guiding and sustaining a free nation through its universal focus on the basic principles of a biblical faith.

Religion, which never intervenes directly in the government of American society, should therefore be considered as the first of their political institutions, for although it did not give them the taste for liberty, it singularly facilitates their use thereof.

The inhabitants of the United States themselves consider religious beliefs from this angle. I do not know if all the Americans have faith in their religion—for who can read the secrets of the heart?—but I am sure that they think it necessary to the maintenance of republican institutions. That is not the view of one class or party among the citizens, but of the whole nation; it is found in all ranks.[2]

What de Tocqueville witnessed and described was the power of a unified Christian national body whose constant appeal was to the word of God, which power formed and sustained the very fabric of American democracy. His logical conclusion was that apart from Christianity, democracy would not—could not—prevail. The mindfulness and pursuit of God's will as manifested in the Holy Bible justified and guaranteed the Republic's existence as one nation under God, otherwise no nation at all.

One only needs to visit the monuments erected in our nation's Capital to verify this tenet. Quotes from the Bible are inscribed in virtually all monuments, and the sacred words and ideals permeate nearly every message of our country's founding fathers. The

Judeo-Christian ethic served as their beacon of light in producing such profound documents as the Declaration of Independence, The Constitution, and the Bill of Rights. Recognizing that God has conferred upon all humans certain inalienable rights yields nothing unless a nation is willing to submit to the Creator's authority. And this they did. How profound is the impact of a united Christian church body.

Harbingers of Spiritual Decay

But now the Bible and prayer are banned from public school. The Pledge of Allegiance to the one nation under God is unheralded and virtually unknown to America's youth. Before our very eyes, within a generation or two, we have witnessed an apostasy from biblical teaching, from the once American way that was energized by the Christian Way.

America is rapidly crumbling. Unless we can unite as a Christian brotherhood and strive for the oneness for which our Savior prayed, we are doomed as a nation. The fall and decline of the great American empire is at hand. We are at the same spiritual crossroads found in Joshua 24:15. We must choose for ourselves this day whom we will serve.

As the lamp of God's word grows dim in the hearts and minds of the American people, we see a proportional moral decadence spreading across the land. We shall pay a heavy price in our own homes, communities, states, and nation. In our state of falling from grace, we no longer enjoy or deserve the respect of other nations. If we refuse to be a unified Christian nation, then to the world we are nothing more than a grossly deformed, decaying, moribund life-form whose spiritual breath is agonal. And so it now seems. God is no longer respected. We are becoming a nation much like the Hebrews during the reign of their judges. "Everyone did what was right in his own eyes" (Judg. 21:25). What is at stake? Everything good. Everything wholesome, upright, and fair. That is what's at stake when Christian unity falters.

The influx of moral decay is crushing us as we drift further away from biblical teachings. We now see infant abortion and even infanticide being praised as good. Pedophilia is touted as healthy and a normal variation of sexual expression. Our children in kindergarten are being indoctrinated into accepting the vilest forms of sexual immorality as normal. Many churches are spiritually crumbling under the pressures of a new godless society, feeling compelled to join the unholy bandwagon for fear of being falsely accused or ridiculed. We don't like being called bigots, homophobes, racists, even sinful, because we stand against the new cultural norms.

What would God say about all this? What *does* God say about it? Scripture is not silent. We yield because we no longer possess the implanted word of God, which is able to save our souls from such wretched filth. Be certain of one thing, The United States of America is now being shipwrecked and shall soon be dashed against the rocks in short order if we do not quickly restore the Christian values that so rapidly produced the most powerful nation in the world. America began as a Christian nation, and because of this, she became a global force for good. If the Bible-based oneness of believers is lost, America shall soon be pummeled to dust. We shall reap what we have sown. The freedom of the American Republic will survive only if we, as a nation, uphold the Bible as our only standard of truth. The quest for Christian oneness is not optional. It is our lifeblood.

America's influence throughout the world as a beacon of light was predicted over 100 years ago by a songwriter named Palmer Hartsough. How prophetic his words seem today.

As Goes America, So Goes the World

As goes America, so goes the world
As goes America, so goes the world
Here where the fight for truth is raging
As goes America, so goes the world
Here where the hosts are now engaging

Chorus

Stand now for righteousness, people so blest
Win thou the victory greatest and best
Lead forward, grand and free, nation of destiny
As goes America, so goes the world
As goes America, so goes the world
Here freedom makes her last endeavour
As goes America, so goes the world
Fails she, and all is lost forever
As goes America, so goes the world
Here lift we Christ, the light bestowing
As goes America, so goes the world
Here serve we God in rightful doing
As goes America, so goes the world
Foremost and highest is her station
As goes America, so goes the world
Leader and guide to every nation

Endnotes

---

[1] Alexis de Tocqueville, *Democracy in America*, Harper & Row, New York, 1969, p.45.

[2] Ibid., p. 292-3.

Chapter 4

Denominationalism: Why So Many Divisions?

Some years ago a young man left home to join the military, eager to discover new worlds far away from his New England home. One day as he sat on a park bench in a small American city in the west, he discovered a little pamphlet that asked, "Are you going to heaven?" As he read the few verses of Scripture about salvation that were cited, his interest was piqued. This message differed greatly from his childhood teachings in the Roman Catholic Church. The words were both comforting and discomforting to him. Could salvation really be that easy? His questions led the man to read the Bible in its entirety, and his life was changed forever. Savoring the words of new life, he now sought Christian fellowship, wishing to obey God and to grow spiritually in the Lord. Naïve as he was and overjoyed at the discovery of this pearl of great price, a full decade passed before he realized that Christians did not always regard true Christians as true Christians. Over time, as he learned of all the divisions among followers of Christ, his enthusiasm waned. "It mustn't be!" he thought. But it was. The house of God was divided. He then knew enough of the Bible to understand the clear message that a house divided against itself cannot stand (cf. Luke 11:17). I am that man.

The New Christian's Dilemma—So Many Churches!

Where does such a new convert to Christianity go? A bumper sticker says, "attend the church of your choice this Sunday," but is that what the Bible says? Which is the right church?

Where can a person in simplicity and purity of heart go to find simple Christian fellowship and share his faith with other brothers and sisters of like mind without being coerced into a denominational mold? History bears witness to such fellowship in sundry times and geographic locations, but it is most likely to be found in places of harsh persecution. For some reason a pure and undefiled form of real Christianity, absent of all denominational constraints, germinates only when our faith in Jesus truly costs us something. Then and only then do we tend to lay aside the pettiness and divisiveness we see operating in our comfortable and complacent fraternal orders.

The modus operandi of the complacent church is exemplified by a peacetime military. On August 18, 1976, two US Army officers were axed to death by North Korean soldiers as they were trimming a tree in the demilitarized zone between North and South Korea. At Mountain Home Air Force Base, Idaho, I was being indoctrinated into the petty politics of a dormant military. Part of my job as an aircraft avionics specialist involved complying with all the petty little rules of Quality Control, or QC. Getting the aircraft operational was secondary to avoiding being written up by QC. Suddenly, when the 366th Tactical Fighter Wing was tasked to support Operation Paul Bunyan in a show of force against North Korea, the first priority was to have all aircraft ready to deploy, ASAP. Quality Control was immediately pulled off the job, and we were told to get all aircraft operational. I had never imagined how efficient, unified in purpose, and effective we as a military team could be in getting our F-111 fighter-bombers launched. The camaraderie was powerfully reinforcing. Despite three grueling days and nights of near constant work and severe sleep deprivation, morale was at an all-time high. We had a mission to accomplish, and by eliminating all the petty nonsense, we were no trifling force. Every soldier did his job without distraction. So it should be with the church.

The apostle Paul teaches us this lesson with boldness. "You therefore must endure hardship as a good soldier of Jesus Christ. No one engaged in warfare entangles himself with the affairs of this life, that he may please him who enlisted him as a soldier" (2 Tim. 2: 3-4). Unfortunately, the army of Christ too often behaves like the peacetime military. We are distracted by trivial pursuits that's only significance is appeasing and dividing the Christian army. Meanwhile the forces of Satan continue to destroy and conquer all around us. To some extent, we are all guilty of neutralizing God's primary force against evil. Whenever we tolerate a "we" versus "they" mentality among the body of Christ, we serve as a barrier to Christian unity. It is time to call denominationalism what it is—a powerful instrument in the hands of the rulers of darkness of this age.

A House Divided

Without delving into a deep discourse on the history of Christianity, we ought to briefly explore the origin and concepts of denominations. When exactly did the church begin to divide? Very likely it began on that splendid Day of Pentecost when the church age was inaugurated. (See Acts 2:1-13.) The seeds of discord were immediately sown when the Holy Spirit empowered the apostles to "speak with other tongues as the Spirit gave them utterance" (v. 4). Scripture clearly states this "speaking in tongues" certainly was not nonsensical babbling. It was an unlearned yet perfect utterance in existing languages of that day, clearly communicating the message of "the wonderful works of God" (v. 11) to all the Jews and proselytes who had gathered for the Jewish feast from many locations across the Mediterranean world. No doubt the message was straightforward, and this miraculous act caught the attention of the hearers in no small way. They were dismayed when they heard uneducated Galileans speaking "each in our own language in which we were born" (v. 8). As soon as the question was asked, "Whatever could this mean?" (v. 12), division began. Why? Because someone was all too eager to offer a wrong interpretation for the unusual event. "They are full of new wine" (v. 13), some mocked. How sad that these accusers would totally ignore the profound import of the message that was authenticated by divine action, and then subvert it with false accusations.

At its core, *division always begins with an interpretation* of the message, or more accurately with a misinterpretation, and this often occurs because of pride. Some may rightly argue that those who suggested the disciples were inebriated were the very same worshippers who might refuse to hear and internalize any spiritual message. But we must remember that this event was a celebration by a holy convocation of God's people, not a heathen mass. Perhaps the problem was that the normal flow of events was disrupted. Can't you hear them? "Wait a minute! That's not the way we do things around here!" The apostle Peter then stepped forward to answer their question about the meaning of this miracle. After he preached this first Gospel message, we are told, "those who gladly received his word were baptized" (Acts 2:41), and so began the Church Age with three thousand new members.

By logical inference, not everyone who heard Peter's message gladly received his word. Imagine the excuses and justifications given by those who rejected his message. We would be foolishly amiss to think anything has changed over the last 2,000 years. Since that time, things have continued to get pretty mixed up.

Even the very word "church" connotes many different things to various people. The fact is, we cannot really "go to church" because we Christians *are* the church. So what's the problem? We now have at our fingertips the entire word of God in one volume, but the same old problem arises at the hearing of these words. The language of the Bible still requires an interpretation. Just as those on Pentecost who wondered after miraculously hearing a mighty message of salvation in their own language, we who read the Bible for the first time also ask, "What does this mean?" Those seeking to oblige us with answers have often done a fine job at muddying the waters of our understanding.

Peter concluded his message on Pentecost by saying, "Therefore let all the house of Israel know assuredly that God has made this Jesus, whom you crucified, both Lord and Christ" (Acts 2:36). How more straightforward could he have spoken? No doubt many walked away angry and disgusted at such a statement, fully knowing this message demanded a response. The sincere in heart reacted much differently. "Now when they heard this they were cut to the heart, and said to Peter and the rest of the apostles, 'Men and brethren, what shall we do?'" (Acts 2: 37).

Contaminating God's Pure Words

Some of the simplest teachings of the Bible have been unnecessarily mystified and rendered unfathomable. In contrast, some of the most profound statements of God have been trivialized or distorted by conjecture or a deceitful heart. When a Scripture passage does not comfortably fit into our denominational box, we have a tendency to gloss over the passage or ignore it altogether. Is this not what we see in the truncated liturgy of Roman Catholicism? But we don't stop there.

In attempts to better define and categorize the treasured tenets and nuances of our cherished sect, we make up new and fancy words not found in the Bible such as acolyte, curate, clergy and laymen, catechism, consubstantiation, diocese, ecumenical, elements, Eucharist, liturgy, sacraments, and other lofty words. Even the words we attribute to Christian holidays such as Christmas and Easter are nowhere found in Scripture. The vocabulary of man-made religion is extensive, but it is not necessarily biblical. We find no such words in the sacred writings.

Once this new jargon is defined and distributed to the biblically illiterate, new requirements for tests of fellowship are introduced along with the fabricated words and concepts. Even in the earliest extra-biblical church writings, deviations and contrivances abound. In the anonymous *Didache* or *Teaching of the Twelve Apostles*, considered to be the "first Catechism," we find subtle and not-so-subtle new teachings beyond what is written in Scripture on baptism, the Lord's Supper, prayer and fasting. For example, the *Didache* instructs followers of Christ to "repeat the Lord's model prayer three times each day," and to fast one or two days before being baptized. It also specifies a priority on the modes of baptism. No such injunctions are mentioned in Scripture and are therefore spurious. All of these impose unnecessary constraints on the elect, and division ensues.

The evolution of the order of Christian worship and organizational rules and creeds has never ceased. Churches are now governed by church boards, not elders, that ratify the new rules of faith and worship, and dictate what members must believe in order to belong. (Have you ever investigated the qualifications of a church board member in the Bible?) Various committees rather than deacons orchestrate specific ministries within the local church body.

The problem with all these contrivances lies not in doing things in an organized way, but in forgetting what the Bible says about church leadership and organization, and considering these "new ways" to be on par with or superior to Bible doctrine. This leads to confusion and effectively dilutes the essential teachings of the Christian faith. When Bible things are not called by Bible names, confusion escalates. Think about how we are all guilty of this to some degree. In Christian gatherings, we don't eat bread and drink wine. Rather we "partake of the elements." We call our love feasts potlucks. Granted, these examples may be inherently benign, but the summation of these subtle deviations is additive in effect. The original purpose of God's design in the Christian community and in gatherings of Christians has become so fragmented and complicated that we can no longer tell what is essential and what isn't. Is this the work of Satan or is it a machination of our own sinful nature? Perhaps both.

Quite interestingly, the genuinely unified crop of the church has always been fertilized by the blood of its martyrs. When Jesus spoke so weightily to the multitudes (Luke 14:27), "Whoever does not bear his cross and come after Me cannot be My disciple," many were likely cut to the heart by those costly words. The sentence of death by Roman crucifixion was not foreign to the listening multitudes. Bearing a cross was something no one aspired to do. Some no doubt distorted His meaning to lessen the impact of His unnerving words. Wouldn't we do the same? How many of those hearers quickly jumped in the shallow end of the spiritual pool and claimed that their cross was perhaps a difficult circumstance in their lives over which they had no control? That is not at all what Jesus meant. His message describes a willful act of lifting up and carrying a burdensome instrument of one's own death. Such is the cost of true discipleship.

This is the true and only response to the message of the cross. Few accept it. But many are pricked in conscience and don't wish to be disqualified. They instead accept a modified version of the hard line in order to assuage their guilt, and they will find a preacher to accommodate them. Perhaps this is why so much of Scripture is trivialized and simple Bible teachings are confounded and distorted. We must remember that the hard (to accept) sayings of Scripture are not intended to incite guilt; rather they are a test of the heart. We are all guilty before God. We all need a Savior. This is the message of the cross. This is also the Good News. What the Bible writers are teaching is that the message of salvation should so inspire us to live with a new purpose and calling that all else is of lesser value, even the duration of our own lives here on earth.

The Cost of a Faith-based Unity

With both joy and sadness we read of countless Christians who rose to the challenge of such a calling. Martyrdom isn't pretty. Throughout history and even up to this present day, Christians have willingly gone to their death out of obedience to Christ. This fact is both sad and inspiring, but perhaps the saddest part of history is knowing that martyrdom often came by the hands of the established church of the day.

In fact, many of the Lord's greatest Bible advocates suffered as they affirmed their allegiance solely to the authority of Scripture. The apostles all (except possibly John) suffered a violent death because of their faith. John Wycliffe, who gave us our first English Bible translation, suffered immensely as he exposed corruption in the churches of England. One of his students, John Huss, likewise committed his life to restoring Christianity to its biblical purpose and design, and his success in calling people back to a pure faith also led to his demise by the established church. As James Murch describes:

His exposition from the Holy Scriptures and his appeals for the restoration of apostolic practices so moved the people who heard him that he was summoned to the Council of Constance to answer for his heresies. There he was seized, cast into a dungeon, and condemned to die by burning. He died with the prayer on his lips, "God give me a fearless heart, a right faith, a firm hope, a perfect love that for Thy sake I may lay down my life with patience and joy."[1]

John Huss took up his cross and followed Jesus. He anticipated death. He knew it was coming. William Tyndale likewise perished by strangulation after being tied to a stake, and his body burned, for the "heresy" of translating the Bible into English. The cost of discipleship, however, is not always so clearly foreshadowed. Take the mass shooting in 2015 at Umpqua Community College in the small town of Roseburg, Oregon, where nine Christians were killed for their profession of Christian faith. The incident was reported by Al Jazeera news network on October 2, 2015, stating that, "The gunman ordered students to stand up if they were Christian and then shot them."[2] A parent of one of the shooting victims reported, "They would stand up and he said, 'Good, because you're a Christian, you're going to see God in just about one second.'"[3] Martyrdom comes in many forms, sometimes unexpectedly, from both within and without the established church.

We in modern America can hardly conceive of martyrdom coming from within the Church again, but only because the American church and America's brand of Christianity has not yet been tested in any big way. Even now as I write these words, Governor Jerry Brown of California has submitted a bill to Congress proposing a ban on all literature that can negatively influence behaviors on sexual expression, namely homosexual behaviors.[4] Since the Bible is clear on calling homosexual behavior what it is—a sinful act condemned by God, then the sale of Bibles would be declared a criminal violation should this Bill pass. It takes no genius to understand where this is going. If California Assembly Bill 2943 were to be approved, then the sale of Bibles in Christian bookstores in California must be shut down.

This is not only an assault on the First Amendment that guarantees freedom of speech. It also is a direct affront to Christianity. As the son of King David writes in Ecclesiastes 1:9, "That which has been is what will be, that which is done is what will be done, and there is nothing new under the sun." Do you consider Christian persecution a thing of the past? Something that happens only in faraway places? Think again. As the homogeneity of Christian union progressively fails, the house of God is weakened, enabling the forces working against Christianity to become ever more empowered. The silencing of Christians by deviant political lobbyists is a real and active threat. They will surely accomplish all of their unholy agenda if we fail to live up to and promote God's holy command to stand firm and unified by the true standard of our Christian faith, the Bible.

Persecution and martyrdom are historically viewed as a sure way of cleansing the elect of Christ. When our own lives are threatened by the words we profess, it is then, more than ever, that we "desire the pure milk of the word" (I Pet 2:2). However, in times of complacency, when all kinds of diluted forms of Christianity prevail, we tend to focus on the "doubtful things" that cause division and strife. Paul, in his letter to the Romans, exhorts us to "receive one who is weak in the faith, but not to disputes over doubtful things" (Rom. 14:1). He gives us some clear examples of such, which many still choose to dispute. When speaking to Timothy, he stresses the need to focus on the essential or indisputable things. "Take heed to yourself and to the doctrine. Continue in them, for in doing this you will save both yourself and those who hear you" (I Tim 4:16).

If Paul walked among us today, he surely would not waste his time speaking of dispensationalism, Arminian or Reformed theology, credos of eternal security or insecurity, other than to correct false teaching. He would not use confusing and lofty words contrived by manmade institutions. He would likely "pursue the things which make for peace and the things by which one may edify another" (Rom 14:19). Our minds are cluttered with a plethora of symbols, forms and ideas with no true origin in Scripture. With so much pseudo-spiritual debris confounding God's plan for a one-body Church, how can we possibly edify the church body? What edifies one segment of the body offends another.

We have formulas, creeds, councils, confessions, movements, statements of faith, and countless "-isms" allegedly propagated to *clarify* the word of God. Each so-called "clarification" brings more obscurity and criteria to further slice the pie of Christian union. A premillennialist may not comfortably consort with a postmillennialist; and amillenialism means what? Certainly not all views can be correct, but for all our theosophy, philosophy and multicolored speculations on the unseen things of God, we have accomplished nothing but shattered any hope of spiritual unity.

However difficult this may be for us to acknowledge, we must accept the fact that all things have not been revealed to us in striking detail in Scripture, and we are foolish and ill-advised to try and clarify or speculate on what we do not know because God has chosen to not reveal it. We are not arbiters of God's design. Our time would be much more profitably spent on those things we do know, and particularly on the things that have been clearly emphasized in God's Word. We ought to speak of things that edify the conglomerate church body by proclaiming only that which God has clearly revealed to us. This is precisely what He teaches us to do—no matter the cost.

Assessing Motives for Defending the Word

Regrettably, in our frail human state we tend to thrive on conflict and one-upping each other. We glory in being right more than in making peace, even when being right in our own eyes may be judged wrong if we had deeper insight and knowledge of spiritual things. As the apostle Paul admonished the arrogant Corinthians, "If anyone thinks that he knows anything, he knows nothing yet as he ought to know" (1 Cor. 8:2). The next time you find yourself contending for a disputed "fact" of Scripture, ask yourself, what is your motive for contention. If you dare to be true to yourself, silence will likely prevail, and rightly so. However, our words must also be fittingly seasoned and appropriate to the occasion.

Discussion in fervent Bible study can strengthen our faith and increase understanding. My point is *not* that we cannot know anything well enough to assert a clear biblical truth. We must always be ready to contend for a biblical faith and to defend clear biblical truths, but we cannot ignore the mandate to edify and strengthen the Christian brotherhood, and particularly the weaker brother. Have you ever been lovingly accepted by a brother or sister in Christ who didn't share all your scriptural perspectives? I have. And on more than one occasion I have humbly confessed that my view was wrong. But how powerful was the mercy and grace they showed to me. I shall never forget these people. I will forever be grateful for their love and kindness toward me, the genuine but genuinely wrong dissenter. I pray that I may never reach the point in my life where I think I am beyond being taught something new from Scripture. The spirit of haughtiness has many subtle forms. It is a deadly sin, killing us spiritually and often causing much collateral damage.

We must recognize and humbly admit that all these manmade categorizations we proudly espouse as principles of Christian theology are mere fodder for confusion. The sin of pride in some of our professional theologians is particularly troublesome because of their uncanny ability to camouflage any chinks in their armor by craftily squelching potential opposition to their "right" dogma by using party lines that must, *ex necessitate*, never be challenged. In fact, we are all inclined to defend our own beliefs, but the church body would be well served to remember the seventh sin that "the Lord hates," as mentioned by Solomon is, "one who sows discord among brethren" (See Prov. 6:16-19).

As we personally accumulate more Bible knowledge, we are increasingly susceptible to the swelling tide of arrogance that so easily ensnares us. Solomon later adds, "The heart of the wise teaches *his mouth* (italics mine), and adds learning to his lips" (Prov. 16:23). As teachers of God's word, we must teach ourselves to control our speech and always question our motives for teaching. We must pray for the wisdom to close our lips when pride begins to rear its ugly head, no matter how justified we may feel in our convictions. The litmus test applied to the gift of teaching is the same as for other spiritual gifts: Does it edify? Does it promote godliness, or does it stimulate arguments? As contenders for the purity of God's word, we must never be cowed into submission when a belief we own is clearly supported by Scripture, but contentious wrangling over obscure passages must be passionately resisted. O scholar, know thy limits!

A spirit of humility goes a long way when we dare to comment and espouse a sure meaning on a difficult passage or a nebulous topic in the Bible. In fact, any author commenting on the sacred words ought to first acknowledge his human weakness and propensity toward error. Albert Outler in prefacing his work on Christian unity beautifully portrays such humility when he writes, "It goes without saying, however, that the cause to which the book is devoted will be served if its errors and misinterpretations are pointed out—and corrected."[5]

With this same humble spirit, we should write or teach very carefully. But we also should always strive for accuracy, knowing that not all readers are equally equipped to correct theological errors. Misinterpretations may be a serious pitfall to the new or weak Christian, and sometimes silence is better. However, silence is difficult when conviction is strong. Let us remember that, however sincere, we may be sincerely wrong. As Paul wrote to his Roman brethren about the Jews, "I bear them witness that they have a zeal for God, but not according to knowledge. For they being ignorant of God's righteousness, and seeking to establish their own righteousness, have not submitted to the righteousness of God" (Rom. 10:2-3).

Are we any different when we alter in any way the message of God by adding to His word in the form of new theological revelations, creeds and tests of fellowship? Is God's word so ineffectual that it cannot stand alone on its own merit? Does not faith come by hearing, "and hearing by the word of God" (Rom 10:17)?

As individuals professing the Christian faith, we must come to terms with our own, sometimes distorted and less-than-perfect, insights and understanding of God's word, plans, and revelation of His will. Perfect knowledge and insight are impossible simply because we are imperfect humans. Because of our ever-longing desire to be right and our underlying insecurity about being proven wrong, we prefer to covetously defend our position rather than acquiesce and reason together.

Recently visiting a small country church, I was encouraged by a Christian brother giving a brief devotion on the Berean spirit (Acts 17). He concluded with a simple question: "What if I'm wrong?" This is the spirit of humility that we should all embrace as we study God's word, more so if we dare to teach God's word. With such transparency, we are likely to hold fast those things of God that are certain, and to keep an open mind and an accordant spirit when reading obscure and difficult passages. To err is human, and to overlook our own errors is equally human. We are sinners, all at the mercy of our Savior. We need Him. He does not need us. His will and perfect plan will ultimately be brought to a certain and flawless conclusion despite all our inadequacies. God certainly honors our genuine efforts to teach, think, and do His will, despite our many flaws. Thankfully, and for our good, His will shall be done on earth as it is in heaven. This understanding should allow us to more easily let go of our insatiable desire to bolster pet doctrines that cannot be solidly defended from Scripture.

I did not discover the impetus for this Christian brother's devotion until after the service. His conclusion was not joyful. What he really meant was, what if *you* (as in, the church's dogma) are wrong?

He confessed that he was coming to different conclusions about various doctrines he had been taught since early childhood. After honestly reading the Scriptures and consequently shedding some of his denominational biases, he became embittered and angry that no extra-denominational views would be tolerated, or even considered in this church. Sadly, this brother never returned to this church again. His concerns were valid. Unfortunately, misguided legalism prevails in many churches. We must always pursue a Berean mindset for the sake of Christian oneness.

The Curse of Denominationalism

Denominationalism is divisive by its very definition and nature. Its selective and biased teaching confuses the biblically illiterate. These dogmas of the various sects separate sincere Christians from one another, and thus weakens the brotherhood of Christ; it bears false witness to the world. It is a stumbling block to the immature in faith and polarizes those self-proclaimed mature believers who conquer and divide in the name of God. Just as with racial prejudice, if a child is raised to believe this division of churches is the acceptable norm and that their denomination is "the best," then they will likely accept this false reality without questioning it into adulthood. God has much to say about all this bickering among His children. It is petty. It is childish. It is sinful.

We who dare to write on any Bible topic would do well to heed the words of Arthur W. Pink who claimed, "Far be it from us to write anything which would discourage the young believer from recognizing and realizing his *dependence* upon God, and his need of constantly turning to Him for wisdom from above, particularly so when engaged in reading or meditating upon His Holy Word."[6]

Unless we continue to depend on this wisdom from above, we shall naturally default to our own self-condemning ways. Denominationalism, with its defining idiosyncratic mandates, is by no means benign. It often leads to spiritual abuse. At best, it creates well-intentioned dragons (the title ascribed to Marshall Shelley's book[7]). When we contend for "our brotherhood," we become spiritual politicians spewing the party line, seeking to swing the vote to our way of thinking. Those whom we sway to believe just as we do become our loyal "party." Then, the most devout of our recruits become lobbyists for "the cause." As this mode of operation ensues, a peculiar form of mathematics occurs: division multiplies. So opposite is this way in comparison to the basic prayer of Jesus for unity among his faithful followers. We must not mistakenly call such behavior loyalty to Christ. In proselytizing for the sect, we are no longer faithful ambassadors for Christ. Evangelizing into a denominational mindset is nothing less than subterfuge, plain and simple.

To summarize, we ought not to confuse loyalty to an esoteric Christian "movement" with following in Christ's steps. The Christian Way is certainly a movement, but "our movement" should never be different from "their movement." The concept of my brotherhood versus your brotherhood is rooted in the spirit of antichrist, not in the Holy Spirit. As the Psalmist proclaimed, "Behold, how good and how pleasant it is for brethren to dwell in unity!" (Ps 133:1).

We are a divided body of Christ because we have not followed God's plan for His universal Church. Denominationalism is not, as some wishful dogmatists claim, just an expression of the diversity and liberty we have in Christ. Jesus never sought to stifle us by taking away our creativity or individuality, but sectarianism is a diversionary tactic to lead people away from the unity for which Jesus prayed. Just as Jacob's coat of many colors was still a coat, a single garment, so are the individuals in the body of Christ also one body. Unity of doctrine and faith must never be destroyed by the worship of false devotion.

Division and unity are, by definition, mutually exclusive. You will have one or the other; never both. Christ alone is Head of this Body. A prophet is not the head. A pastor is not the head. An organizational church board is not the head. Government is not the head. We must not grasp this concept only by intellectual assent. We must live it daily. What are the criteria for membership into your local church? The question, what must I do to be accepted by a local body of believers is plainly answered in Scripture. If any criteria greater than those delineated in Scripture are prerequisites, then your church is hindering the purpose for which Christ died. If your church espouses that which is not clearly mandated in the Bible, then your church is at odds with the Lord's prayer to His Father in John 17. Blessed is the church that models the purpose, mandates, and practices of the Church that Jesus Christ alone founded. Blessed is the Christian who seeks to unify the body of Christ according to God's rules, and His alone.

Endnotes

[1] James DeForest Murch, *Christians Only*, Standard Publishing Company, Cincinnati, 1962, p. 13.

[2] "Nine dead in shooting at college in US state of Oregon," October 02, 2015, aljazeera.net, accessed on November 30, 2018.

[3] Ibid.

[4] Chris Woodward and Billy Davis, "Vote delayed, but coming next month, over AB 2943," July 10, 2018, OneNewsNow.com, accessed on August 03, 2018.

[5] Albert C. Outler, *The Christian Tradition and the Unity We Seek*, Oxford University Press, New York, 1957, p. x, xi.

[6] Arthur W. Pink, *Interpretation of the Scriptures*, Baker Book House, Grand Rapids, 1972, p. 8.

[7] Marshall Shelley, *Well-Intentioned Dragons*, Word Publishing, Dallas, 1985.

Chapter 5
Things That Divide Us

If we ever hope to see progress in the merging of all Christian believers into a unified body, we are obligated to candidly explore the real issues that separate us. This involves asking the hard questions, such as how exactly does one church that claims loyalty to Christ differ so much from another church that affirms the same allegiance? What specific practices in one denomination so ardently offend those of another denomination, and why? Why can a gathering of Christians in any one locale not readily join hands with Christians in another place without feeling like an outsider? Obviously, something is terribly wrong. We all have the same Bible, the same inspired words protected by the Holy Spirit, the same object of worship. These articles of contention must be investigated head on to seek a sincere resolution. We must put these daft points of contention to rest once and for all, and the score must be settled by the words of Scripture alone.

Credibility of Creeds

Before exploring specific doctrines and church practices that divide us, we might wish to first consider what unites us. What things are essential, leaving no room for compromise? Can we agree on anything? If you were to make a list of the bottom-line criteria in declaring another to be your brother or sister in Christ, what would you write? Take a few minutes and write down what you determine to be the bare essentials of what it means to be a Christian. Now, go a little further and ask a few of your trusted friends in your congregation to do likewise. Then share your answers with one another. Do you notice any differences in your lists? If so, then who is right, and how do you know? Should you defend your position? How far should you go in defending it? Okay, stop there. That was a dangerous thing to ask you to do.

What you may or may not have realized is that you just formulated a creed, a statement of what you consider the essentials of the Christian faith. If you're totally honest with yourself, you may have left out a few important things on your list that someone else in your group included. You also probably would take exception to a few statements others listed. This is how it works in church councils, in synods, in legislative bodies that meet to consult and determine church matters. In fact, this is exactly how the "Apostles' Creed" was formulated. This Creed, although having wide appeal among Christians, is actually a misnomer. It most certainly was not a document written by the apostles. It came about from some early Christian leaders who found themselves forced to respond to an infiltration of false teaching.

However good their intentions, they established a pattern for other statements of faith. Now, virtually every existing church has a "We Believe" statement to define who exactly they are and what beliefs must be held as a prerequisite to membership. What's wrong with that, you may ask. Nothing necessarily—if it truly does not conflict with Scripture. It may even accomplish some good, in light of some resurgent heresies, such as rejecting the virgin birth or the deity of Jesus Christ. But a creed statement still is an addition to the Scripture. Paraphrasing any biblical doctrine risks distorting the message. It also creates an opportunity to emphasize one doctrine over another, thereby subtly branding one's own version of fundamental beliefs. Why do it?

Did you ever consider that, in essence, when you made your list you might have added to or taken away from the word of God? And what did you choose to leave out? Omissions can have as much impact as affirmations. If leaders of a church add a statement of faith that must be subscribed to as a prerequisite to being accepted as a member of a local church, then such leaders are patterning themselves after the pseudo-Christian cults who always use the Bible *plus* some additional writing as their basis for truth. Be it another book, a prophet, or some other medium or agency to convey their "essential truths," anytime God's word is not allowed to stand on its own authority, rest assured, false teaching is sure to follow. The Bible says very clearly that this is wrong. Paul told the Corinthians to "learn in us not to think beyond what is written, that none of you may be puffed up on behalf of one against the other" (1 Cor. 4:6).

As we sit comfortably in our pews listening to a sermon, we are always potentially at risk of hearing some degree of false teaching. Paul warned Timothy, "evil men and imposters will grow worse and worse, deceiving and being deceived" (2 Tim. 3:13). For this reason he exhorted Timothy from many angles. "Take heed to yourself and to the doctrine" (1 Tim. 4:16), "And the things that you have heard from me among many witnesses, commit these to faithful men who will be able to teach others also" (2 Tim. 2:2). "Remind them of these things, charging them before the Lord not to strive about words to no profit, to the ruin of the hearers. Be diligent to present yourself approved to God, a worker who does not need to be ashamed, rightly dividing the word of truth" (2 Tim. 2:14-15).

Paul urged Timothy to "continue in the things which you have learned and been assured of" (2 Tim. 3:14), reminding him that "All Scripture is given by inspiration of God [literally, *God-breathed*], and is profitable for doctrine, for reproof, for correction, for instruction in righteousness, that the man of God may be complete, thoroughly equipped for every good work" (2 Tim. 3:16–17).

Timothy was never instructed to produce any new creed or mission statement. He was directed to "the Holy Scriptures, which are able to make you wise for salvation through faith which is in Christ Jesus." If a man of God is thoroughly equipped by the God-inspired Scriptures, then he needs no foundational creed, no extra-biblical statement of faith to solidify or define his faith in Christ. The Holy Spirit needs no assistance from us to improve upon His work. What every Christian does need is fellowship with other Christians. In short, the whole body of Scripture is our creed. We are united as a spiritual family through the Bible, and it alone.

Vilifying Themes

Now let's explore some specific topics that divide us, issues that malign one group of believers in the eyes of another. Ask any believer how God will culminate the history of mankind and you likely will get a wide assortment of viewpoints. The same is true if you solicit beliefs about what happens after we die. What is heaven going to be like? What will be our eternal state of affairs?

Unlike the consummation of the ages, Christians tend to claim ignorance about many details regarding our heavenly abode, although the Bible offers about as much details of the afterlife as it does the end of ages. Why are we so willing to grill one another on eschatological details, while allowing free reign on our concept of life in the new heaven and new earth? Perhaps Randy Alcorn, who wrote a rather comprehensive volume about our final destination, is correct when he claims that Heaven suffers as a subject precisely because it comes last, not only in theological works but also in seminary and Bible college classrooms.[1] In fact, he suggests that so much time and energy are spent on eschatology that no time is left to discuss the finer details of heaven, where we shall spend the overwhelming majority of our time. Anyone who has ever attended a Bible college or Seminary would be hard pressed to disagree with him.

Have you ever debated the subject of miracles? What purpose did they serve, and do they still happen? Any discussion on this topic must start with *your* definition of a miracle? Should we consider answered prayer a miracle? Or is it just an answered prayer? And what is the purpose of suffering? Is hell a real place where people are actually tormented forever? How could a loving God create such a place? Many Christians find these questions very intimidating for a number of reasons. One reason may be simply because biblical answers are not readily available or clear. Another may be because pre-conceived notions are strong, and arguments are likely to fester when each defends his own viewpoint across denominational or theological lines.

Much distress occurs because of misunderstandings or ignorance of what the Bible actually says about these subjects. Or our concern may derive from the teachings of our specific brotherhood (which, of course, is tacitly indisputable). Discovering the deeper things of God requires much effort in searching out the Scriptures, and even after diligent study we will not always agree. Must we have a full consensus on all things theological? How do we begin to reason together about such things amidst all the partisan animosity?

As the apostle Paul evangelized the Mediterranean world, he exclaimed, "I determined not to know anything among you except Jesus Christ and Him crucified" (I Cor. 2:2). This was his raison d'être, his primary focus as he tried to win souls for Christ. He never forgot that primacy of purpose. Not that he had nothing else to teach or knew little else, but the doctrine of the redemptive work of Jesus at the cross was his central theme. All else was subordinate. When Jesus declared, "It is finished," the climax of the history of mankind was marked by its most significant event, right there at the cross. The message of the cross, however, is often completely obscured by other messages of denominational importance. We seem all too eager to major in the minors while ignoring the countless millions of people who are hell bound. Arguments often arise from preconceived views about what took place in the beginning of time (the Creation account) and what will happen at the end times. We also are all too willing to dispute so many other less consequential doctrines between the beginning and end times. Why? Has it yielded any positive fruit? If our goal is to merely prove a point, then we are shackled by our pride.

This is not to say we should have no lines in the sand. Boundaries of true Christian brotherhood must necessarily be defined somehow. A Muslim is certainly not akin to a Christian, despite their claim to worship the same God; neither is an atheist. One would think that the definition of a Christian would be straightforward enough. No Christian can logically declare himself a spirit-brother to an enlightened Buddhist or a pantheistic Hindu. But we also fall far short of claiming that anyone who avows the Bible as his rule of faith and practice is a Christian, do we not? What difference does it make if one brother is a premillennialist and another has postmillennial views? Certainly both cannot be right. Some will claim that neither is right. But does this influence the character of his soul? Maybe. Shall his view condemn him on the Day of Judgment? Probably not. Does it hinder evangelism? Not likely, but it could.[2]

In contrast, what does it matter if one regards Jesus as God incarnate or if He is considered the first of God's creation? Well, this matters a great deal for it goes to the heart of what differentiates Christianity from other religions or beliefs. Of necessity, we do have some fundamental beliefs that define the Christian faith to maintain the integrity of the flock. If not, then the word Christian becomes meaningless.

But the "in-between" doctrines, for lack of a better definition, are the ones that most often cause a great deal of bitter fighting among Christians. This is what Paul was indirectly saying when he highlighted the doctrine of "Jesus Christ and Him crucified" as a chief theme of his ministry. Paul was expressing the one unifying principle of all followers of Christ, that Jesus is the Messiah, the Savior of the world, the only Way by which we may receive eternal life. This is the crux of the cross!

Whenever we delve into argumentation about lesser doctrines, we risk division of the body and the eternal lives of countless souls. My contention is not that we should never deal with any other Christian doctrines, but that we tread gently and with the purpose of building Christian character and leading one another toward a greater maturity in our Christian faith. We are no more saved by our knowledge than we are by works. What then shall we do? Shall we lovingly ignore or render void the weightier matters of Bible doctrine for the sake of unity? Or should we stomp the soapbox of every biblical truth for truth's sake? How far should we go to defend a truth at the expense of maligning or alienating a brother or sister in Christ? Exactly where is the dividing line between a divider and a unifier of the Christian corpus? These are not easy questions to answer.

Two Camps

Essentially, we have two camps competing for Christian unity: the love camp and the truth camp. Both camps make strong arguments, and indeed both have necessary tools instrumental to building unity in the church. In reality, one camp simply cannot exist apart from the other. This principle is clearly elucidated by the aged and seasoned apostle John in his letters to the "little children," that is, his spiritually younger Christians. John declares that we must genuinely love one another (I John 3:23) and that we must also know the truth (II John 1).

The two camps should obviously be joined as one, as both are necessary. This is not a one or the other proposition. It is symbiotic—both camps go together and thrive upon one another. In John's second letter he supports this by saying, "This is love, that we walk according to His commandments. This is the commandment, that as you have heard from the beginning, you should walk in it. For many deceivers have gone out into the world who do not confess Jesus Christ as coming in the flesh. This is the deceiver and the antichrist" (II John 6-7). If anyone doubts that he is referring to doctrinal truth, read verses 9-11. "Whoever transgresses and does not abide in the doctrine of Christ does not have God. He who abides in the doctrine of Christ has both the Father and the Son. If anyone comes to you and does not bring this doctrine, do not receive him into your house, nor greet him; for he who greets him shares in his evil deeds." Now those are some serious admonitions. Love one another, but don't for one second tolerate unsound doctrine.

In the quest for solidarity as a universal body of Christ, the love camp extremists would argue that love conquers all, to the exclusion of all Biblical truth. Love is certainly a powerful wall crusher and accomplishes much in toppling the bastions of sectarian hatred that grates many souls. However, love apart from truth becomes so mushy as to disavow the Christ-given gift to the Church, which is the entirety of His teachings and examples in the pages of Scripture. These churches welcome anyone who claims to be a Christian without testing their faith. Here enters false doctrine.

Without the biblical revelation we would have no Christianity. Christians are followers of Jesus, called to be set apart from the world by abiding in the words of our Savior. These words are given to us only in the sacred writings. In Charles Sheldon's classic work he raises the question, "What would Jesus do?"[3] In order to rightfully answer this question, or more pertinently the question, what would Jesus do if He were me in my present circumstances, we are obligated to first answer the question, what does the Bible say? If we ignore that question, then we are apt to stumble into the ever-fallacious justifier of "The Spirit led me" or "God spoke to my heart," without any basis for heavenly guidance from the Divine Book.

I am in no way attempting to negate the power of the Holy Spirit working in us. Truly He empowers us and help us in our spiritual walk, but never apart from the very teachings that the Holy Spirit Himself directly inspired men to write. The problem with the "God told me" argument is that such assertions are often tenaciously held despite being in direct conflict with scriptural teaching. Such claims also cannot be tested, except by scriptural validation. The Holy Spirit, being God, cannot and does not contradict Himself. We are certainly advised to test all things (1 Thess. 5:21), and the basis for all testing of truth claims is the body of holy writings—the Bible. All conflicting claims must be regarded as spurious and untrue. "For God is not the author of confusion but of peace" (1 Cor. 14:33). If a man speaks contrary to a clear teaching of Scripture, then "let God be true but every man a liar" (Rom. 3:4).

Confusing Doctrines

So what do we do when Christian brothers and sisters are hung up on those "in-between" doctrines? First, we should define the term. An in-between doctrine is any spiritual teaching not considered a test of fellowship but leads to argumentation, confusion, and division. For example, one may propose that all pets go to heaven. Another disagrees. Is this really worth fighting about? A heretical teaching clearly contradicts Scripture and should be refuted. Many "in-between" doctrines, however, are either assumptions or opinions based on unclear texts, or ineptitude in understanding clear biblical teaching. The list of divisive doctrines is likely endless. One church insists Christians should not drink alcohol under any circumstances, in any amount. Another says we must worship on this or that day. Some insist that eating meat was never God's will.

Others claim that we will surely be raptured before that great time of tribulation.

What about "speaking in tongues?" Well, that leads to another discussion of miraculous gifts. Is rational discussion on this topic even possible? When discussing this issue we must sort out the non-miraculous gifts. All believers are fully convinced they are right and hold faithful to their convictions. Many are so convinced of their positions they would almost stake their salvation on it, although salvation itself is not the issue.

Such stubbornness only embitters the soul, particularly when blind faithfulness is contrary to sound Bible teaching. These false tests of brotherhood guarantee that we will never come together globally as a unified family of God. In a way very similar to the Crusades of the Middle Ages, every denomination is on its own crusade to defend its version of the truth against all others. With so much confusion these days on a vast number of biblical precepts, we are doomed to forever remain divided unless we can somehow inspire a Copernican revolution[4] about the importance of Christian unity, whereby Christ is the center of our universe. Confusing doctrines usually originate in poor scholarship, wrong interpretations, and from human pride. We can put the confusion to rest, but not without a proper approach to the Bible. If we blindly hold fast to our petty dogmas without a true testing of our claims with Scripture as the measuring rod, then the things that divide us shall grow exponentially.

The Preacher's Dilemma

Before a new preacher is hired, he is carefully examined regarding his qualifications, his lifestyle and his beliefs. The greatest concern is not so much that his beliefs align with Scripture, but ensuring they align with traditional beliefs of the denomination. Where he trained, and by whom, bears more weight on whether he will pass the doctrinal test than his actual command of scriptural knowledge. His interview will consist of a series of questions that are not intended to test his Bible knowledge but rather to identify his interpretative biases.

The typical church board involved in hiring the new preacher must know that he is first and foremost "one of us." If he satisfies this "doctrinal" requirement of the sect, he must then demonstrate his charisma and crowd appeal. After all, numerical growth is important. Can he put a smile on each face in the congregation? Can he preach without offending? Will he sufficiently entertain a crowd so they will want to return to hear more next week? Finally, if he meets the socialite test, his lifestyle will be briefly evaluated. This means he must be a conformist to the ways of the denomination. He must certainly speak in tongues and fully support it. Or he must not. He must sympathetically hear the cry of the LGBTQIA (lesbian-gay-bisexual-transgender-queer-intersexual-asexual) movement and defend it. Or he must fully renounce it. He must agree to not dress the wrong way, act the wrong way, or introduce any new way of thinking that would disturb or discomfort any members of the church leadership. This is every preacher's dilemma.

How stifling is this reality to the spiritual growth of the church. A preacher of any denomination is at risk of unemployment if he takes exception to any mainline denominational dogma, regardless of what the Bible may or may not say about the subject.

Sadly, his livelihood is at risk if he deviates at any time from the party line or displeases in any way those who financially support him. When Christ is not Head of the church, then both the paid preacher and the assembly are not permitted to test all things and hold fast to what is good, as Paul instructed the Thessalonians to do (I Thess. 5:21). The preacher's dilemma is that he must tickle the ears of those who write his paycheck. He must forever concern himself with pleasing men first with words that flatter the composers of the sectarian doctrinal creed. "We believe thus, so you are enjoined to preach thus," they say. Pleasing God by faithfully preaching His word is subservient to the partisan edicts. Denominational traditions are never to be challenged by a divisive preacher with the audacity to prick our consciences or challenge our thinking with solid biblical truth. Those possessing the power of the coin insist that the preacher take no liberties of conscience, however biblically based, and continue to earnestly meet all their demands, however unscriptural. Keep us in our comfort zone—that is the tacit message of the institutional VIPs.

Dare we call this behavior what it really is? It is nothing less than a form of mind control, a bushwhacking of the kind of Christian fellowship that God intended for his followers. Have you noticed what happens after such unmerited termination of a preacher? Many churches divide further. Yes, church division often results from disloyalty to a faithful preacher of God's word.

The Cost of Faithful Discipleship

For obvious practical reasons, many a hired preacher has submitted to such ungodly authority, hoping to beat the odds of a three-year ministry before being tossed aside for another ear tickler. Stability of lifestyle often demands compromising one's integrity by preachers whose flocks are shepherded by wolves in sheep's clothing.

On the other hand, God has always given us true heroes of the faith who seek to call us back to God's plan, regardless of the personal cost. I mentioned three of them earlier. John Wycliffe labored at giving us our first English translation of the Bible. He felt strongly compelled to expose the errors of the church based on what he read in Scripture. This was risky business in his day, and he paid a high price for his back-to-the-Bible views. Not only was he threatened with loss of his livelihood and excommunication, but he also was threatened with the loss of his own life because the Roman Catholic Church outlawed the reading of scriptures by the common man, under penalty of death.

For the same reason John Huss, a student of Wycliffe, was burned at the stake. Some authors and preachers still seek to revitalize the church in modern times. Lawrence Richards, for example, purposes in his book to "examine the church as revealed in Scripture" and "to reconstruct local church life to fit biblical patterns."[5]

The problem we now face is that through the ages we have deviated so far from the biblical pattern that it is well-nigh impossible to recognize it, let alone accept it. Pity the rare zealot who proposes a return to a biblical model for church life where unity might prevail. He likely will be quickly and harshly squelched, being told that his ideas are too radical, that the church has evolved from its past simplicity.

Though his ideas may fully align with the apostolic model, he will be declared an unrealistic fanatic. The coordinated attack by leadership would be quickly launched: "How dare he suggest doing things God's way! These are modern times, and we know better than God how to run His church." While these words may not be expressed verbatim, the idea is strongly conveyed by their words and actions, and the result is the same. Manmade tradition supersedes real Christianity. When sound unity principles fail, the church is further weakened, and the destroyer prevails.

The church in America is at a crossroads. If we choose to continue in our current amoral trends and weak traditions, we will continue to be safe; but impotent. If we choose to abide in Christ and diligently follow His teachings, we shall face great personal risk. Unfortunately, we live in an era of religious liberalism that progressively loosens the biblical construct of what defines a church, and even a Christian.

We have arrived at a point where we now see appeals for accepting gender fluidity among Christians. God's gender roles fashioned into the design of His creation of the church, and marriage, have been stowed away in the relics trunk. Suddenly, under pressure from the new social norms, homosexuality is becoming acceptable in many denominations. What for ages was declared unholy and sinful is now fashionably acceptable. Some churches are now appealing to a gender-neutral God.

In 1973, Karl Menninger exposed the spiritual landslide that occurred in the turbulent sixties when the test of truth suddenly became based on feelings and was no longer defined by Scripture.[6] Those radical times called for going with the flow, questioning authority, and for disavowing all absolutes. From the effects of this wretchedness we have never recovered, and decades later we are still slide down its slippery slope.

With this spirit of rebellion permeating the churches, how then can we even begin to deal with teachings such as miracles, the indwelling of the Holy Spirit, Christian baptism, the laying on of hands, a bodily resurrection of the dead and eternal judgment? So much confusion exists on these topics that most teachers would rather avoid any discussion of them rather than risk creating a scandal. How ironic that many of these subjects are called the *elementary* principles of Christ (Hebrews 6:1-2). If we cannot in good faith broach these basic principles of the faith, then how shall we go to maturity in our spiritual journey? How can we ever battle the forces of evil that seemingly smother us in the present age? Of course, the answer is always the same—return to the Bible for a spiritual awakening. And by all means, put on the full armor of God (Eph. 6:11-17), for the battle is raging.

A new evil has infected the church since the moral landslide of the sixties prevailed, one that challenges the livelihood of not only the preacher but church leaders themselves, and subsequently the whole church body. In the Bible, we read many accounts of false teachers and divisive brethren in the local church who were named and directly disciplined. In 3 John 9 the apostle John directly exposes and renounces the prideful Diotrophes who refused to accept John's apostolic authority and teaching. Jesus Himself exposed the apostle who would betray Him. A church elder following their examples in the twenty-first century is likely to face a lawsuit for defamation of character. Could this be a reason for the moral laxity and spiritual decay of the church? What church leader is willing to place his neck on the chopping block to satisfy the God-given mandate for church discipline? What has happened to solid biblical church leadership?

Cursed Undiscipline

Even good church discipline cannot ensure unity. The Bible teaches that we have no guarantee that peace and harmony will prevail in the local church. Having the same traditions, a similar Bible translation, even a mature and wise eldership is not enough. Declaring that the Scriptures are inerrant and infallible does not prevent churches from dividing even though all members may agree on this vital premise.

Trouble arises when we fail to recognize our own fallibility. The Holy Spirit inspired the biblical writers, but He did not inspire any of us in our *interpretation* of the inspired writings. Every preacher standing before a congregation and expounding on any Scripture passage is capable of speaking in error. The only possible way to *not* introduce an error is to simply read the Bible text, nothing more. Even when adhering to sound doctrine, the textual critic might challenge the Bible expositor by saying his interpretation is flawed. And it very well may be. Even the most disciplined preacher is not immune from errors of interpretation. An implausible defense against such errors is the claim that the Bible interpreter, whoever it may be—any member of the church—is "illuminated" by the Holy

Spirit to discern all errors of interpretation. More will be said on this later as we deal with methods of interpretation. For now, let it be said that no mortal may honestly claim that such illumination is infallible. Were it so, we would not be divided into denominations.

Such propositions of illumination do not bolster but rather discredit the work of the Holy Spirit. The very fact that highly educated and God-fearing scholars among Jewish, Roman Catholic and Protestant denominations, who ardently support each of their own views, attests to the assertion that whatever is meant by the term illumination, it cannot mean that the Holy Spirit protects us from errors of interpretation.

Somebody has to be wrong if more than one rendition of a passage is offered. Begging full integrity and humility of our souls, we must confess that we are all subject to misgivings about what God meant to say when it comes to certain Bible passages and topics. We also must concede that some hard sayings in Scripture *do* exist, and that not all things have been revealed to us. No matter how diligent our study, how passionate our zeal to know God, and regardless of how faithful our desire to rightly interpret Scripture, we shall all fail to some degree. Some facts will remain hidden to us all. We shall never know the author of the book of Hebrews. We were never told how many half-brothers or half-sisters Jesus had, and even if we were, what difference would it make? This is a great question to ask yourself before you open a Pandora's box the next time you wish to challenge someone on his beliefs about the end times. How will such a debate make me a stronger Christian? Will it build the faith of my brother or sister, or could it weaken or destroy someone's faith unnecessarily? These are questions worthy of some meditation because, although I strive to ask these questions, I do not deny that we may have some well thought out reasons to assert a particular viewpoint. But we also must forever ask ourselves if Jesus would make an issue of these beliefs. As the sayings go, think before you speak, and look before you leap. Causing a sibling in the faith to stumble is a very serious offense in God's eyes, and we will be judged by what we say and do. Need I really cite a Bible reference?

As a final thought regarding things that divide us, I've often wondered why God in His infinite knowledge and wisdom revealed His will to us in written form. That He inspired the likes of farmers and fishermen, kings and tax collectors, strong men and weak men, weak-minded and strong-headed persons riddled with all manner of serious character flaws is beyond my comprehension.

Perhaps He wished to prove how much He could do with so little, and He certainly has proven His point. But rather than have all these scattered inerrant original documents and letters that were later copied and spread across the globe, why didn't he just zap this information into our brains directly? Why all the fuss? He seems to have chosen a dangerously tortuous path full of obstacles and hindrances to accomplish His purpose of revealing Himself to us. And then He prayed for unity.

The apostle Paul tells us, "Work out your own salvation with fear and trembling" (Phil. 2:12). When I see the fragmentation of His church body through the ages, even to this present day, in my foolish speculation I want to ask God, "Couldn't you have done this differently?" That is another question that shall never be directly answered this side of glory. Or maybe it already has been answered in Scripture. Deuteronomy 29:29 says, "The secret things belong to the Lord our God, but those things which are revealed belong to us and to our children forever, that we may do all the words of this law." In the New Testament we read, "Oh, the depth of the riches both of the wisdom and knowledge of God! How unsearchable are His judgments and His ways past finding out!" (Rom 11:33).

We must submit forever to God's ways in the knowledge that we cannot even begin to understand how and why He has allowed history to unfold as it has. Despite all my foolish pondering, I give thanks to God that He is in control of this world and of His church body. And I am glad that He is doing things His way, not yours or mine. Whatever His design for the church, it is a perfect plan. Nothing could be better. And when the final curtain drops, the history of mankind shall reveal it.

Endnotes

[1] Randy Alcorn, *Heaven*, Tyndale House, Carol Stream, Illinois, 2004, p. 9.

[2] The eschatology wars are a cause of much division among denominations, and many scholars would vehemently argue that one's belief system of the end times does influence our every day thinking and spiritual life. The point here is that the process of redemption, i.e., salvation through the blood of Christ, preempts in importance the details of the summation of the age of mankind. If you feel a need to argue this point, then my point has been clearly elucidated about things that divide us.

[3] Charles M. Sheldon, *In His Steps*, Barbour and Company, Westwood, New Jersey, 1984.

[4] For those without basic knowledge of astronomy, Nicolaus Copernicus gave us our present model of the Solar System, placing the sun at the center of a group of planets orbiting around the sun.

[5] Lawrence O. Richards, *A New Face for the Church*, Zondervan, Grand Rapids, 1981, p. 8.

[6] Karl Menninger, M.D., *Whatever Became of Sin*, Hawthorn Books, New York, 1973.

Chapter 6

The Crux of the Disunity Problem

Spiritual and physical separation of churches doesn't just happen. Much like an airplane crash, the disaster results from a sequence of events rather than just one mistake, oversight or malfunction. Churches that divide and separate on issues of doctrine, protocol and petty grievances do so for a number of reasons. Internal division starts as a sequence of deviations from a healthy protocol, such as the aircraft checklist, in aviation lingo.

This process then proceeds to external division, or denominationalism. If one major flaw could be cited as the chief source of division among a church body, my contention is that the ruling authority in the church missed the mark by failing to practice a Bible-based form of leadership. From this one defect arise all other woes that eventually lead to a fractured church. Bad teaching, errors of interpretation, semantics, lack of vision, quests for popularity, poor stewardship, worldly influences, and all other difficulties in the church stem from faulty leadership that is not modeled according to God's instruction manual.

Leadership Amiss

Since the Creator of our universe has seen fit to convene members of His family in the design of local churches, it behooves us to pay close attention to the pattern or blueprint He gave us. Many church leaders have put forth much effort in creating the "perfect" worship experience. The larger the church and the wealthier its members, the more grandiose the worship service.

In the twenty-first century church, the gospel message seems to be served on every sort of platter imaginable in hopes of bringing in more people to hear God's word, or more likely to further augment church revenues. Millions of dollars are spent in attracting bees to the hive. We now have gourmet coffee, professional musicians, popular preachers, and high-tech multimedia presentations to lure in new believers and new seekers. If possible, we bring in big-name speakers who require a gratuity rather than request a love offering. We have sports teams and church camps and special retreats. We have small church groups and large church groups, and we send our youth on exotic vacations designated as "missionary trips" where they can expand their horizons.

The most prosperous of these church models are lifted up on pedestals for all to emulate, and these successful entrepreneurs are in high demand to teach their skillful church building craft to the less prolific church assemblies, so they might follow the franchise model and also reign triumphantly one day. Of course, this is all done in the name of church outreach and evangelism. Disneyland uses the same tactics. Unfortunately, despite the magnificent outward success of these few ecclesiastical monuments, most local churches continue struggling for their life to attract new members. Recent history has shown us that church attendance dwindles rapidly when the novelty of the amusements wear off or the magnetic charisma of the current preacher is no longer present. Many claim that the church in America is dying, and current statistics support this observation.[1] Go into a small church service on any given worship day and you are likely to find a geriatric population, devoid of youth and new converts. Too many of these small churches, representing the majority of Christian gatherings across America, are a generation away from their own funeral service.

If you talk to any worshipers from either the mega-churches or the small country churches, they really aren't all that different. Whatever attracts people to high-entertainment churches seems not to inculcate any obvious spiritual leverage or lasting benefit over the smaller churches. The hearts of people in the smaller congregations may be a little more personable, but also a lot more stiff and dogmatic in temperament due to having a weightier influence within a small group of people.

While passing judgment on any of these churches takes no effort from an outsider, we on the inside must ask ourselves whether or not we are worthy of the criticism. Let's face our problem squarely: the contemporary church is in trouble. We have strayed far from the biblical pattern of communal worship. God had a certain plan for His church, and much of the disunity we see today has arisen from ignoring the first-century church model, from which we glean the principles and purpose of God's design.

This model focus much on character building, on virtues, on evangelism, and on holy living rather than entertainment and fancy trappings. But it also establishes for us a pattern for worship, leadership, sharing, discipline and the preaching of sound doctrine. This blueprint has been boldly and capably expounded in John MacArthur's book, *The Master's Plan for the Church*. He analyzed the structure and function of the church assembly, according to the Bible. Then he acutely identifies the top-down leadership problem when he states, "Some contemporary church leaders fancy themselves businessmen, media figures, entertainers, psychologists, philosophers, or lawyers. Yet those notions contrast sharply with the symbolism Scripture employs to depict spiritual leaders."[2]

This truth is well-stated. In contrast, one famous Bible scholar worded it this way: "My speech and my preaching were not with persuasive words of human wisdom, but in demonstration of the Spirit and of power, that your faith should not be in the wisdom of men but in the power of God" (1 Cor. 2:4-5). The sum total of worldly glitter and verbal prowess is mere chaff compared to the power of the gospel message spoken clearly and plainly. All else is but a distraction.

The present American church model is far more a product of the industrial revolution than a Bible-based entity. As MacArthur further states, "The design of the Christian church is not to have a professional preacher financed by laymen who are merely spectators."[3] Nowhere in Scripture do we find a concept of clergy or laity, nor a single ruling "pastor." Sadly, the very words that describe church leaders in Scripture are so grossly misunderstood that the average Christian has no concept of true biblical leadership.

The Bible uses the words elder, shepherd and overseer interchangeably, and a multiplicity of leaders existed in every local first-century church. In the modern church model, leadership has typically defaulted to the combined ruling by a single hired pastor and the eminent church board, the latter always being more powerful than the lone pastor. Decisions are made by vote, applying Robert's Rules of Order to moderate negotiations and matters of the church. This has become the accepted norm in the great majority of churches. Whatever happened to the power of the Holy Spirit?

Few Christians recognize this as a corrupted leadership model because they do not understand the scriptural definitions of an elder as a mature, Bible-wise servant-leader; a pastor as one who shepherds the flock; and a bishop as one who oversees the spiritual growth, safety and unity of the church body—and that all three are a reference to the same church office held by more than one temporally and spiritually mature, male, Christian church member. This fact is self-evident when comparing the qualifications of a bishop in 1 Timothy 3:1-7 with the qualifications of an elder in Titus 1:6-9. The apostle Peter integrates all three terms when he exhorts the *elders* to *shepherd* the flock and serve as *overseers* of the body (1 Pet. 5:1-2).

Some will wince at reading these words, deeming such a model archaic, chauvinistic, and unnecessary. If this strikes a chord with you, then you are a victim of false teaching and biblical illiteracy, and a proponent of division. As one Greek scholar has asserted, "The language of the Church had better be the language of the NT. To proclaim the Gospel with new terminology is hazardous when much of the message and valuable overtones that are implicit in the NT might be lost forever."[4] If the very design of church leadership is grossly skewed, how can church unity ever be maintained? If we reject the Master's plan for His church, the ensuing structural flaws will eventually bring about a weak and ineffective body, regardless of the size, location or focus of the church.

Some church leaders claim that times were very different in the first century and the form of governance then practiced was necessary for a church in its infancy. They regard the structure of church leadership and worship *then* as being only historically relevant *now*. They thus assert that we need new ways of shepherding churchgoers and attracting new members in our modern times lest the church otherwise fail. They claim the methods utilized by the first-century church are impractical and outdated, no longer effective. Nothing could be further from the truth. Both the methods and principles of the Christ-ordained church are efficacious for growing the local church into a spiritually mature and unified body. Nothing less will suffice to engender individual spiritual growth and thereby maintain a vigorous oneness of the church family.

What we need for a successful church—and I'm talking success based on God's perspective—is to build each local church exactly as God ordained it to be. We ought to use his prescribed design, methods, mandates and verbiage. Anything less is spiritual mutiny. No manmade contrivances can possibly improve upon the spirituality, effectiveness, or harmony of the Christian assembly as ordained by God.

We must acknowledge and confess that the aristocracy in most local churches are tacitly elected more because of their business prowess, high-technology acumen, or people-attracting charisma rather than the biblical requirements set forth for elders and deacons. In smaller churches we are more apt to find the patriarch or matriarch of a family calling the shots on how to run the church. Considered the best of patriarchs is he who is able to appeal to a democratic leadership style. All is decided by popular vote. Votes may settle the color of carpeting but are anathema when challenging Christ's church anatomy. Both methods of leadership negate the power of God's word and the power of the Holy Spirit to do the good work that results from a Bible-centric church leadership model.

The Circus Effect

Coined "The Greatest Show on Earth," the Ringling Bros. Circus entertained the world with their novelties of talented exotic animals, bizarre exhibits, and stunning performances. Their dazzling exhibitions were most impressive, attracting hordes of entertainment-starved people all across America. Such are the tactics of many churches today.

Allow me to create a hypothetical scenario. Imagine yourself one Sunday morning walking into a ten-thousand-member church popularized by all the frills and thrills of entertainment, food and beverages, comfortable seating, a delightful ambience, and music to stir the deepest emotions of the human soul. On this particular Sunday morning, a simple dry-board sign greets each church member entering the facility. It reads: "Change of worship service."

An attendant informs the congregation that there will be no music or special performances today. All the video and sound systems will be turned off. The bistro café is closed, and no food or drinks shall be served. To make matters worse, the air conditioner is turned off and the southern California summer heat is sweltering. A disconcerting rumble is heard in crescendo as the well-attired entertainment seekers flow in and find their place among wooden folding chairs in place of the familiar plush padded seats. The illustrious dais and pulpit have been replaced by a cheap metal music stand. The colossal video monitors mounted on each side of the 60-foot-tall sanctuary are black. Aside from the disgruntled murmurings, an unnerving silence replaces the upbeat instrumental prelude typically resounding in the theater by this time.

As the preacher approaches the music stand, he smiles warmly and welcomes this shaken but expectant brotherhood of believers. "Today, I've decided on a little change in format. For starters, let's have an hour of prayer. Then we'll share some of our struggles together, and maybe pray some more. After this, we'll read from God's word. Did you bring your Bibles? And then we'll break bread and drink wine to remember our Lord's sacrifice to save our wretched souls from just condemnation. After that, I'll speak a few words that might encourage you to live a little more like Jesus."

By this time ten thousand jaws are gaping wide.

Okay, bad joke! (Or is it?) But let's assume this agenda is exactly what unfolded over the next two hours. After a closing prayer, the minister informs the members that this will be the new nature of worship gatherings for the next year.

By the end of the service, something very different has transpired in this gaggle of worshippers. Some actually stormed out early in their indignation. Others are grumbling, outwardly expressing their disappointment at what they feel is such an unprofessional lack of showmanship. A few bolder members are sarcastically asking if their preacher has been tipping the bottle lately.

But others, saying little or nothing, feel a strange sense of renewal, something unexpected but empowering. As the weeks ensue, attendance rapidly dwindles. How many seats will be filled by the end of the year is uncertain, but as more seats are unused with each passing week, a new and tightly knit unity is forming in the fellowship of those who remain.

Although this is a hypothetical situation, real-life parallels of this scenario have actually occurred. When a popular or renowned preacher moves on or retires, some churches dwindled to only a few loyal members, while the majority defected and sought a new source of entertainment. Of course, they would never use such language. They would call their moving on a quest for a church that better attends to their spiritual needs. Whatever the motive, a church is divided in the process. Booming churches have become ghost towns virtually overnight after the circus has left town. This raises the question, was this true fellowship? Or was it just entertainment? Even though the remnant in such churches may struggle financially, a church that functions in a biblical manner is much more likely to be a dynamic body of Christ followers whose purpose is not to be entertained but to be challenged to offer themselves as a living sacrifice to the Lord.

The Best Worship Model

When they came together, the early Christians had few of the many distractions we have today. The focus was on the cross. Their meetings were purposeful and consumed in prayer. Love was strengthened through sharing, and the souls of disciples were inspired by attentively listening to the reading and preaching of God's word. A Jesus-centeredness of gathering was ensured by breaking bread in memory of Jesus's atoning death on the cross. Its effect was powerful.

In present-day churches, many people would immediately stand up and walk out if the entertainment were cancelled. What sort of person would stay after the forsaking of all the hype? When considering the two types of gatherings, which group would likely be more unified, the amusement seekers or the God seekers? If the show were canceled in your church, what would you do?

Don't get me wrong, I love listening to beautiful music and talented singers. I enjoy listening to an inspiring preacher. Sipping on coffee is heartwarming, and comfortable chairs and an HVAC system are much appreciated. The point I'm making here is that if we do not model our worship gatherings according to God's design for His church, then its spiritual depth will never exceed that of a puddle.

Any circus can gather a crowd, but God's style of worship creates committed and unified disciples—true followers of Christ. About this time, some of you are probably shaking your fists, thinking it's not the methods that are important—it's the message. Others might retort that the early church model was transient; it was only intended to get the early church rolling. Now that things are up and running it has evolved into something bigger and better, so we've got to do things differently. Is that so? If the Hand of Providence is sustaining the "new methods" of worship, then why are so many churches failing? Why is America in a moral land-slide? What has weakened the influence of twenty-first-century Christianity? And why are conversions to Christianity at an all-time low in America?

We are projected to see a decline in the number of Christians in the United States "from more than three-quarters of the popu-lation in 2010 to two-thirds in 2050."[5] I assert that the feebleness of the American church is a product of our refusal to follow both the methods and purpose put forth by the inspired writers. While we are allowed much latitude in our methods of worship, we are likewise exhorted to include certain elements of worship in order to accomplish the *purpose* of the church, which is to lead people to the real fountain of youth. Jesus spoke of it to the Samaritan woman in Sychar who was drawing water from Jacob's well. He told her, "whoever drinks of the water that I shall give him will never thirst. But the water that I shall give him will become in him a fountain of water springing up into everlasting life" (John 4: 14). This is the nourishment we seek in worship.

Yes, following God's plan is essential for solidarity among all true Christian disciples. The banner of Christian discord flies high mainly because of our own refusal to follow that divine scheme. God points out in Romans 14 that our *methods*, such as acceptable foods or day of worship, are not nearly as important as our *purpose*. But our purpose is also realized in God's protocol for group worship. We now have arrived at a point in history where what is beholden and acceptable in worship to one local church or Christian is a malediction to another.

Something is terribly wrong. All kinds of biases and presuppositions dictate the elements of our church constitutions and worship formats. Semantics and the collapse of logic further obscure our understanding of God's will for a unified church across the globe. Because of our own human pride, we judge and criticize each other's methods without even referencing what the Bible says about worship. Even as we each appeal to the very words of Scripture, we inconsistently apply rules of interpretation, if we even know the rules (and the overwhelming majority do not).

While the chief cause of church dissonance appears to derive from faulty leadership, the quintessential disunity problem likely has its roots in our own selfish pride. Solomon sums it up very well when he admonishes, "By pride comes nothing but strife" (Prov. 13:10a). Who of us can deny that our sectarian discord results from strife about irrelevant minutia, and this disharmony from pride? Pride rears its unsightly head whenever we refuse to humble ourselves before the Almighty. But how can we edify others toward godliness without committing offense? We do it by first humbling ourselves. Genuine humility requires a pure heart. We can promote humility in others only after squelching pride in ourselves. Humility is displayed by a slow temper, an absence of harsh words, and a life whose ways flesh out a servant's heart by concrete acts of kindness. A servant seeks to please his master, and our Master is the Lord.

If we are ever to progress toward unifying the church, we shall accomplish it only by getting back to our sole source of true unity—the Bible. But unity through Scripture can prevail only to the extent that the Bible is properly interpreted.

Two essential ingredients exist for a genuine nondenominational, God-desired unity to prevail: a pure heart and a right interpretation. If hermeneutics is the science of interpretation, then what might be said of the art of interpretation? The scientific method is explicitly based on observation of events that are predictably reproducible. When the scientific method is applied to biblical interpretation, then one would expect only one meaning from any given text. But this is precisely what is not found when we read the Bible commentaries of many scholars. How can this be? Euphemistically, we might say that each scholar is applying his art of interpretation to the science of interpretation, which more directly stated is inherently a battle between the sinful mindedness of man as he struggles with the true intent of God's word.

When the Holy Spirit guided the words of those who penned the original autographs of Scripture, He intended it to say only one thing. That one thing was meant to be understood in one way. But understanding of Bible truth is directly dependent on a humble submission, with full integrity to the science of interpretive method. One might propose that strict adherence to the science of interpretation *is* the *art* of interpretation, if there truly is such a thing. The most skillful artist would be he who minimizes his own will and maximizes the will and intention of God as he interprets. Said another way, Maier quotes Procksch who regarded "the battle between God and man taking place in the very act of biblical interpretation."[6] As this battle is waged, various interpretations inevitably arise, even with passages of Scripture that are most lucidly written.

Given the fact that we often turn to religious scholars for guidance in how to interpret the Scripture, and that only one interpretation at most can be correct, we are left with the serious quandary of determining who among the scholars is giving the right interpretation when all have impressive credentials. Such scholarly guidance is often invaluable, but scholars often disagree. Equally worthy of investigation, then, is the degree of humility with which each scholar approaches his study of God's word. Of course, gathering information on the character of an author is not easy work, and perfect understanding of the intent of another's heart can never be fully discerned by another mortal. One cannot quickly assess the heart of man (Jer. 17:9), but as a general principle—not exclusively—the more dogmatic and forceful the author's views of Scripture, likely the more prideful is the scholar's heart. We should most keenly awaken our sensitivities to the destructive nature of pride, particularly when it comes to Bible interpretation. And when reading any Bible scholar's commentary, we should do so with full awareness of his discernible biases.

A Right Interpretation and A Pure Heart

We also must regard arriving at the correct interpretation of Scripture as an act of spiritual discipline. When an accurate interpretation is made and understood, then we are speaking the same things and are of like mind. This is clearly God's desire for us. Regrettably, many Bible readers place a low priority on sound interpretation, and so anything goes. In His profound commission,

Jesus did not say to go and make converts to Christianity; He said to make disciples. There's a big difference.

Becoming students of God's word is serious business. Diligently striving for accuracy of interpretation ought to be a foundational teaching in the making of disciples. Unfortunately, most new converts to Christ are poorly instructed in the full meaning of conversion. They are rather persuaded to "make a decision" for Christ. This is hardly discipleship. New converts naturally bask themselves in the blessedness of receiving the gift of eternal life—as they should. But not knowing the cost of discipleship, they are satisfied and complacent in their new condition of being saved from the much-deserved wrath of God, being unaware that "as newborn babes," they should "desire the pure milk of the word" so that they may grow into maturity (I Pet 2:2).

Paul encouraged the Christians in Philippi, "Work out your own salvation with fear and trembling" (Phil 2:12). These words explicitly declare that such a workout is no simple task. How else can we work out our salvation than by reading, studying and heeding God's word? This, in my estimation, is an essential ingredient of becoming one as a body of Christ: a right interpretation of God's message, followed by a doing of His word.

Please hear what I am *not* saying. No man has full knowledge of God or even His written words. When difficult or disputable passages arise, perhaps a conclusion of "I knoweth not" is better than a faulty dogmatic interpretation that produces disharmony in the church body. The fundamental message of the path to salvation and instructions in Christian living are quite clear, however. As previously stated, such basic teachings can be easily understood by any reader with average intelligence, and it takes a scholar of renowned selective bias and semantic influence to confuse the import of such passages. Hence we need *both* a pure heart and a right interpretation to bring about unity in the Christian body.

Looking back through church history, we see the development of a systematic theology formulated by rules of interpretation. Various schools of thought evolved in the post-apostolic era, some of which were severely flawed. When the apostles themselves spoke, and when the authors of Scripture wrote, their teaching was authoritative because the Holy Spirit protected the accuracy of their written words. However, when the last apostle took his final breath, this divine inspiration ended. From this point onward we are left with a full written account of those things God has deemed essential for the development and completion of our faith. Revelation is complete.

As the science and art of interpretation later evolved through uninspired men, many excellent principles were laid down to equip us with an ability to properly interpret Scripture in a way that minimizes error while maximizing our ability to rightly divide the word of God. Yet those who most avidly promulgated good methods of interpretation often themselves blatantly ignored their own rules of interpretation whenever the right hermeneutic interfered with the wrong preconception. Ramm mentions of Augustine's hermeneutics, "As magnificent an effort as this appears, it is disheartening to realize how far short in so many instances Augustine came. There is hardly a rule he made which he did not frequently violate."[7]

Such willful disregard shall never do, knowing that personal bias always divides us and leads us away from the truth. Rules are useless if not faithfully and consistently observed.

What follows in subsequent chapters is 1) an exposition of how and why we deviate from sound interpretation due to our own human vulnerabilities, 2) the essentials of sound interpretation, and 3) concrete ways in which we can attain to unity in our local churches, in our Christian communities, and in the universal Christian body.

Endnotes

1 Frank Newport, "Church Leaders and Declining Religious Service Attendance," September 7, 2018, <news.gallup.com>, accessed on April 07, 2019.

2 John F. MacArthur, Jr., *The Master's Plan for the Church*, Moody, Chicago, 1991, p. 15.

3 Ibid., p. 106.

4 Nigel Turner, *Christian Words*, Thomas Nelson, Nashville, 1981, p. viii.

5 "World Religions Population: Growth Projections, 2010-2050." April 02, 2015, <pewforum.org>, accessed on April 04, 2019.

6 Gerhard Maier, *Biblical Hermeneutics*, Crossway Books, Wheaton, Illinois, 1994, p. 24.

7 Bernard Ramm, *Protestant Biblical interpretation*, 2d ed., Baker Book House, Grand Rapids, 1970, p. 37.

Chapter 7

Where Do We Begin?

I must confess that I truly do not understand how we as a conglomerate body of Christians could have become as divided as we are today. The extent of our division attests to Satan's power to destroy us. Do you remember when you first read the Bible with all eagerness of heart to find out what God was telling you? The words were inspiring and motivating, challenging you to put aside former lusts and meaningless pursuits in exchange for a far better way of life. But as the years unfolded, the impact of those words somehow began to lose their power.

When we dig deeper for meaning, more questions arise. At some undetermined point in time, the quest for knowledge may become its own end, leading us to forsake all the *doing* that previously renewed our hearts and minds. We can so easily get caught up in the search for some new discovery about God that we forget to faithfully follow God. Obedience is often neglected in favor of accumulating knowledge as an end in itself, much like like the Athenians who "spent their time in nothing else but either to hear or to tell some new thing" (Acts 17:21).

When no doctrinal stone has been left unturned in the quest to eke out every contrived meaning from Scripture on every topic, are we the better for it? Or have we only pursued such insights in

87

order to stand a cut above the brotherhood at large? The resultant kaleidoscopic mishmash of denominational beliefs has created a meaningless and impotent force of so-called Christians who are obsessed with privy knowledge that yields nothing in the way of building true disciples who will change the world. Today, we have far too many Christians who know *about* God but do not *know* God.

In the hundreds of Christian books I have read over the years, I simply cannot comprehend how and why so much of Scripture is simply ignored, misrepresented, or seemingly has no bearing or influence upon whatever Christian topic is being addressed. I fully realize that such a statement can easily be perceived as being arrogant, but in all humility, I have searched my soul to find an answer to the question of why we are so divided. Is it because we have no fear of God? Do we not consider the Bible as truth? Or do we consider the Bible to be only historical fiction with some nice suggestions for us? Have we too long ignored the weightier matters of Scripture and focused merely on the niceties of outward worship? Unless we can identify the real causes of disunity among us, we are doomed to face the consequences of this flawed theology and Christian lifestyle.

The Fear of God

I once believed that the deepest roots of church division stemmed from a lack of a genuine fear of God. I still believe this, only more so now. After all, isn't this the ultimate cause of all evildoing in the world? We can always expect the worst in a society that does not fear God. Abraham did. When Abimelech asked Abraham why he claimed Sarah as his sister and not his wife, Abraham truthfully stated, "Because I thought, surely the fear of God is not in this place; and they will kill me on account of my wife" (Gen. 20:11). Right or wrong, it was rational thinking.

The Bible contains over three hundred references to fearing the Lord, and the definition of this fear should not be diluted to meaning a mere reverence or respect. When Jesus said, "Do not fear those who kill the body but cannot kill the soul. But rather fear Him who is able to destroy both soul and body in hell" (Matt. 10:28), we can assume with all certainly He meant all-out trepidation, a dread and terror of horrible and eternal consequences if we deny Him and His message of salvation. Imagine the gripping fear we would experience if we were suddenly sentenced to death by burning at the stake. Burning is is likely the most painful death a person could experience. But Jesus is saying, if I may paraphrase, "That's nothing at all compared to a spiritual death."

A healthy fear of God actually affords us much benefit. Solomon tells us, "The fear of the Lord is the beginning of knowledge" (Prov. 1:7), and King David wrote, "The fear of the Lord is the beginning of wisdom" (Ps. 111:10). The Bible should be the primary textbook studied at every higher institution. Such words imply that we are doomed to a life of ignorance and folly if we do not fear the Lord. Likewise, a Christian who has no fear of God also has no respect for God's will to be done, including His will that we may all be one. The ultimate conclusion is that he who does not fear God does not respect His message—His written word.

Many sincere Christians have been taught that we need not fear God because God is love (1 John 4:16) and because God desires all to be saved (1 Tim. 2:4). While this is true, they conveniently forget that our God also "is a consuming fire" (Heb. 12:29). Consequently, we suffer from either a lack of discernment in knowing God's word, or from a willful disregard of His design for the church. This sort of fearlessness is anything but heroic; it is an act of disobedience to God.

Many emotional pains in our personal lives, and in the local church, are a direct result of not fearing God, resulting in not doing things according to God's design. Rather than spending our time and energy on thoughtfully discriminating and understanding God's truths, we focus more on doing things our own way. We choose to make our own golden calf to worship rather than hearing what God really has to say, and this always gets us into trouble. Whenever we reject God's best, we always pay a price. A healthy fear of the Lord is a good starting point in approaching Scripture. Asking God with all fear and reverence, "What do you really mean to tell me?" is a great way to begin unraveling the mess we have created in our schismatic theology. If the fear of the Lord is the beginning of knowledge and wisdom, then it will serve us well in knowing God's truth in Scripture. This is our starting point as we investigate the path toward a biblical plan for oneness.

"I Think" Theology

A common approach to group Bible study is for the teacher to read a passage of Scripture and then ask the open-ended question, "What do you think that means?" or "What does this verse mean to you?" This technique is a great icebreaker, and it certainly gets people talking, sometimes vehemently. It may encourage some to contemplate what they think and believe, and gives a voice to those eager to share their feelings about the passage.

Responses will likely vary based on one's life experiences, depth of Bible knowledge, current events, personal biases, and degree of personal faith. Unfortunately, such a method of study may also lead to deviant and highly subjective explanations that do little or no justice to the intent of the biblical author. If a Bible study teacher seeks opinions from all hearers based on each one's personal understanding of a Bible text, errors of interpretation may be allowed so as not to offend a good-hearted and well-intentioned fellow Christian. When unfettered opinions are solicited, a can of worms can then be opened. The number of opinions on any given Bible text may well approach the number of participants in the study group. Who then shall decide on the "right opinion" without possibly wounding the soul of those with "wrong" opinions? And by whose authority is the verdict of truth declared? This appears to be the most egregious error of Bible study. It betrays the author. Nothing is more damaging to unity and to arriving at a sound biblical interpretation than "I think" theology.

The truth is, what I think or what you think regarding any holy text is unimportant and irrelevant compared to what the inspired writer meant for us to understand. Sound interpretation of God's word is tantamount to unifying the church. That is to say that we must faithfully and diligently strive to make every word, every purpose, every guiding principle and intent of the author, mean exactly what God intended it to mean. We must assume one and only one meaning.

Only then can we receive the wisdom of God and become faithful doers of the word. Any other meaning leads to a false and unfaithful application of the purposeful intent of the passage. Our just query of Bible knowledge and its utility must not lead us to ask, "What does this mean to you?" but rather "What did the author mean by his words?" Some might argue that such an approach squelches the Holy Spirit, but this itself is an example of "I think" theology. We must remember that the Bible is intrinsically a work of the Holy Spirit. Peter the apostle tells us, "No prophecy of Scripture is of any private interpretation" (2 Pet. 1: 20), and therefore my or your interpretation of Scripture is invalid if it does not reflect the Spirit's intended meaning. The sacred writers composed their works under the full protection and guidance of the Holy Spirit. If we *think* something is so, then our beliefs should coincide with those of the inspired writers. Valid conclusions about the meaning of any passage of Scripture can be reached only by making the Bible say precisely what the writer intended to say. Creative improvisation and fancy parlance are never constructive, always divisive.

The apostle Paul instructed Timothy to remind Christians "not to strive about words to no profit" (2 Tim. 2:14). But how does one discern what words are unprofitable? Who decides what might ruin the hearers? Paul gave us the answer when he warned Timothy to be most discerning as "a worker who does not need to be ashamed, rightly dividing the word of truth" (2 Tim. 2:15). The Scripture gives us words to much profit when they are rightly divided. A correct interpretation protects us from the malignancy of heresy, which goal is always to conquer and divide. This mandate given to Timothy is critical for us all in order to preserve the doctrinal unity essential for godliness. It requires all diligence and discernment when reading the Bible and listening to any message from any speaker. Our goal must always be to "shun profane and idle babblings, for they will increase to more ungodliness. And their message will spread like cancer" (2 Tim. 2:16-17).

Like Hymenaeus and Philetus "who have strayed concerning the truth" (2 Tim. 2:18), such is the way of the cultist and false prophet. His chief goal is to persuade his hearers to disengage the brain. Stop thinking; forget what Scripture says; just listen to what I tell you and blindly believe it. Once this is accomplished, the cultist has full reign over his victims' souls. The only escape from such a spiritual death and pending judgment is to seek a blank slate interpretation of the Bible, which is addressed in the next section.

Many former cultists have testified about their means of escape by assenting to put aside all their cultic teaching and read the Bible with an open mind. This prima facie look at Scripture attests to the power of the Holy Spirit to accomplish His good work in the genuine seeker of God. Contrary to a blind sectarian allegiance, we are expected to "have the mind of Christ" (1 Cor. 2:16). We are told to diligently study God's word, to write it in our hearts and minds, and to search out the Scriptures to evaluate the veracity of all that we are taught from any and all sources. Be the message from a Bible study or from behind a pulpit, we should always search the

Scriptures to determine the truth of all teaching. In the end, opinions do not matter. We should not think so highly of our own opinions that we blindly choose ignorance over truth. We also should test all doctrinal claims (even our own) against what Scripture actually says, no matter how esteemed the speaker or author.

Blank Slate Approach to Interpretation

A monumental barrier to discerning Bible truth is personal bias. Imagine a person who knows nothing of God opening the Bible for the very first time. He has a Bible before him, sans all Bible aids, and nobody to explain its meaning. Beginning with Genesis, he reads about the creation of the world and concludes that God created the heavens and the earth in six days. He completes reading the first five books of Moses (called the Pentateuch) and understands that God has rules and expectations for His people, and that the consequences of sinful disobedience to God are devastating.

As he proceeds reading through the period of the judges of Israel, he discovers that good and bad leaders can determine the fate of a nation. The poetic books then speak wisdom to him in a different way, giving much practical advice and exposing the struggling hearts of even kings. He concludes that everyone needs God. Working through the books of the Major Prophets (Isaiah through Daniel) and then the Minor Prophets (Hosea through Malachi), he reads many things that are hard to understand. But unlike the Ethiopian eunuch who did not comprehend the then incomplete writings of God, this novice has access to the completed New Testament.

As he reads the Gospels, he comes to understand how Jesus is the fulfillment of things predicted long ago—the long-awaited Messiah. The way of salvation is revealed and proclaimed. He reads the critical question in Acts 16:31, "What must I do to be saved?" He too wishes to be saved. In his mind, he is asking the same question: What must I do? With eager anticipation he is searching for the Bible's answer. This reader would be a student of "blank slate" theology, having no preconceived notions about what is essential in the process of conversion.

Blank slate theory, called *tabula rasa,* proposes that the human brain at birth is devoid of all rules or instructions for processing data from the experiences in life. In modern psychology, blank slate refers to a universal innate potential not constrained by genetic factors. This theory is commonly attributed to the English philosopher John Locke, although the concept is believed to have originated with the early Greek philosophers.

While the theory has been largely refuted, I use the term here to designate an open-minded approach to reading the Bible, free of all outside influence. Of course, this is never completely possible since a brain that has developed enough to read has already formulated some notion about the way things are. But nothing can liberate us more from the curse of sectarian bias than a "What saith the Scriptures?" quest for God's revealed truth in written form. The student of blank slate Bible study understands that the Bible stands alone as the supreme authority on all matters necessary for salvation and knowing God's will. Moses proclaimed to the Israelites, "You shall not add to the word which I am commanding you, nor take away from it, that you may keep the commandments of the Lord your God which I command you" (Deut. 4:2). This injunction has never changed throughout the entire Bible. The apostle John clearly warns us at the closing of his revelation. "I testify to everyone who hears the words of the prophecy of this book: if anyone adds to these things, God will add to him the plagues that are written in this book; and if anyone takes away from the words of the book of this prophecy, God shall take away his part from the Book of Life, from the holy city, and from the things which are written in this book" (Rev. 22:18-19).

How ironic that so many Christians dare to venture into speculation about this revelation, seemingly oblivious to the foretold consequences of altering the message with false knowledge. Open-mindedness refers not to speculation about what is not revealed, but to the blank slate of a heart that is eager to hear and accept the revealed word of God in its pure form.

This is not to say there is no value in having a knowledgeable teacher for instruction. The study of Scripture is hard work. Many theologians have spent much of their lives excavating the deeper riches of Scripture. We have been blessed with astounding archaeological discoveries that have affirmed the integrity of the biblical record. We can better understand old manuscripts through the painstaking efforts and scholarship of linguists.

Despite all the erudition, however, God tells us through the prophet Jeremiah, "You will seek Me and find Me when you search for Me with all your heart" (Jer. 29:13). Finding deeper meaning from hallowed words requires a diligent and sometimes grueling journey into the history and culture of Bible times. It commands an understanding of grammar and syntax, and of literary forms. The astute and faithful interpreter of divine words is no sloth. But neither must he be an astrophysicist. We must never forget that "the fear of the Lord is the beginning of knowledge" (Prov. 1:7) and also "the fear of the Lord is the beginning of wisdom, and the knowledge of the Holy One is understanding" (Prov. 9:10). A college degree is not a prerequisite to knowing God, but fearing God is.

When God reveals His nature to us and His will through words (called special revelation), we are obligated to respond. With a virginal curiosity, we should ask, what does He say? Only then are we properly empowered to answer the corollary question, what shall I do? The answer to these two questions requires only the availability of the Old and New Testament writings and a true heart for God, apart from all manmade declarations of what is essential. Beware the scholar with an agenda! Imagine what conclusions we might reach with our own understanding as we read Scripture plainly and simply for what it says, without donning the spectacles of preconceived ideas that have already shaped our skewed theology. This is blank slate interpretation.

Getting a Handle on Scripture

Practical wisdom teaches us that in our humanity, we all doubt God at times. Doubt is not rejection, however. We often fail to understand all that is written by God due to the numerous cultural, linguistic and historical barriers that obscure our ability to comprehend. To further complicate our journey of knowing God, we often put up our own defenses when reading a difficult saying in Scripture because we fear what God may require of us. Such barriers to understanding God's word can stunt anyone's spiritual growth.

One way to help us to understand and correctly interpret His word is to find those passages of Scripture that are so solidly indisputable and straightforward that nobody can question them. I call these Scripture "handles" because we can read these words and have no doubt about their meaning. We can grab onto these verses and know confidently what is being said, without any doubt.

Consider for example the emotionally charged chapter of 1 Corinthians 14 that deals with spiritual gifts. The correct interpretation of this chapter requires some historical Bible knowledge, spiritual maturity, grammatical integrity and some rigid interpretive (hermeneutical) skills. To "rightly divide" this word of God, a blank slate frame of mind is also essential if we are to get at the true intent of the text. All kinds of abuses and misinterpretations—and thus divisions—stem from a poor understanding of these words. However, contained within these words are some utterly simple, undisputed teachings that tell us very clearly what God desires us to know. One such handle is stated in verse 26: "Let all things be done for edification." Another is found in verse 40, whereby Paul concludes his discourse of how things ought to be done in public worship. He summarizes by stating, "Let all things be done properly and in an orderly manner."

Okay. Whatever we do in our Christian gatherings, all things should have the purpose of strengthening and encouraging one another, and they should be done in an organized way. If any confusion ensues from such verses, then it stems from some root of ungodliness, or at least an unwillingness to do things God's way. But when the Bible clearly explains a universal teaching about how we should act or how something should be done, or defines a concrete principle or truth, we have no room for disputation.

Many such handles are present throughout the Bible. Only deceptive worldly reasoning could muddy these waters, and then only in the most feebleminded or insincere of heart. God has declared the "disputer of this age" a fool, having worldly wisdom (1 Cor. 1:20). We should glean these firm teachings in Scripture, things that are indisputable, and then build upon them.

The Role of the Holy Spirit

In the beginning of any textbook on Bible interpretation, you are likely to find some sort of "disclaimer" about the role of the Holy Spirit with regard to our understanding and interpretation of the written word of God. Christian scholars refer to this role as the "illumination of the Holy Spirit." This illumination or enlightenment is usually touted as being essential to "quicken" the mind in order for a passage of Scripture to be properly understood. The protagonists of Holy Spirit illumination claim that without this enlightenment, the Bible can never be properly understood. Such a claim suggests that the entire Bible is a parable, requiring a special discernment to understand its words. This is a somewhat dangerous proposal, as it implies that without the aid of the Holy Spirit a person cannot read the words with any meaningful understanding. Such a claim simultaneously negates the power of inspiration in protecting and guiding the Bible authors as they wrote words intended to reveal the very will of God.

As a more youthful student of Bible interpretation, and having trudged through several textbooks on hermeneutics, I was quite amused by this passing homage to the necessity of this Holy Spirit illumination in the authors' introductory remarks, only to then see the same authors proceed with a highly detailed discourse on all the rules of language comprehension that must be carefully followed and mastered in order to get at the right meaning of God's message. No further mention of Holy Spirit illumination was made in most of the books I had read.

Gerhard Maier deals with this subject at length early on in his work on interpretation, but he warns of potential abuse by concluding that an exaggerated emphasis on pneumatology "can threaten a proper understanding of revelation and shows disdain for methodological rigor."[1] Does he mean by this that the Holy Spirit's work of illumination is flawed, or is he suggesting that the Holy Spirit rewards diligent study of hermeneutics? His pattern of discussion was typical of most scholars. After introducing and affirming the concept of illumination, he then qualifies it, and thereafter ignores it. Roger Chambers observed this same paradigm.[2]

I must raise this issue of concern specifically to debunk the false claims of some misguided believers who insist that their varied interpretations of a passage of Scripture are correct, of necessity, by each person's claim to Holy Spirit illumination. Each of them held a different view or interpretation of a passage or Bible topic. If the same Holy Spirit is illuminating each interpreter's understanding of Scripture, then something is amiss. Either the Spirit is in error, or illumination cannot possibly refer to guidance into the proper interpretation of the written word. Without regard for any of the rules that fill the pages of hermeneutic textbooks, a tyrannical departure from sound doctrine prevails. Such a claim to having been enlightened in Scriptural interpretation is pure casuistry, and it betrays the role of the role of the Spirit as Helper and Encourager. The Holy Spirit does not protect the accuracy of our Bible interpretation. The Holy Spirit also does not lead us into error. Jack Cottrell opines that illumination is a false doctrine for three convincing reasons, one of which I have already discussed.[3] The Holy Spirit's influence is nowhere to be discovered in opposing interpretations. Someone has to be wrong. Cottrell asserts that we often willfully misinterpret Scripture because we do not want to conform our lives to its true meaning.[4] This strikes at the core of our problem with diverse interpretations.

On the other hand, I can readily sympathize with these fellow Christians. Accurate interpretation is hard work. Faithful living is even harder. Given that I had labored and toiled countless hours to memorize a whole array of rules in order to become a somewhat disciplined and accurate interpreter, I frankly wondered… if God wanted us to have all this knowledge, then why couldn't the Holy Spirit, for all His supposed "enlightenment," just zap all this Bible knowledge into my brain so that I needn't bother myself with all these rules! Some thirty plus years later, I still have no way of measuring my degree of illumination, and I only jestingly entertain any concept of progressive illumination. The rules still apply.

Failure to abide by these rules of interpretation still leads to the same empty babblings that they did in the first century AD. I continue to see ample evidence of discordant teaching among those who claim Holy Spirit illumination. This erroneous belief in illumination is a tragic reality in our churches, and the Holy Spirit can hardly be blamed for such travesty. We are in no position to question the ways of God. I would be a fool to challenge God about why He uses us mentally frail and sin-flawed people to lead others to Christ. My arrogance would be further exposed if I called God out for revealing Himself to us through the written word rather than innate knowledge. While I have no solid answer to these questions, apparently God assigns meaning to our human efforts. We find God when we diligently seek Him. We spread the Gospel when we faithfully obey Him. We yield spiritual fruit when we submit to a higher calling that does not naturally belong to us. We really do work out our salvation with fear and trembling, and our sincere efforts return a high yield in spiritual formation.

So, the question remains, what exactly *is* the role of the Holy Spirit when it comes to our understanding of Scripture? What gift does He bestow upon us, and how does He assist us? Unfortunately, many well-intentioned Christians who seek to honor the Holy Spirit by claiming illumination actually slander Him by espousing their wrong scriptural interpretations. If we are to accurately define the Holy Spirit's role in our understanding of Scripture, then perhaps we should begin with a survey of how the Spirit has acted in the past. We must also allow for a biblical definition of the word *illumination*.

The Greek verb *photizo* (Strong's #G5461) is used in various forms by John, Paul, and the author of Hebrews to describe a shining of light upon the spoken or written word, so as to enhance the understanding of the conveyed message. In a general sense, John describes this source of light as the Messiah, "which gives light to every man coming into the world" (Jn. 1:9).

This enlightenment refers to a *knowing about* the Messiah, not an intimate, spiritual knowing Him. Clearly this general knowing does not necessarily lead to an intimate fellowship with God in a relational way. The apostle John elucidates this point when he tells us that this Jewish Savior "came to his own, and His own did not receive Him" (John 1:11). The goal of Jesus's entering our world was "to make all see what is the fellowship of the mystery, which from the beginning of the ages has been hidden in God who created all things through Jesus Christ" (Eph. 3:9).

This general bringing to light is quite different from the deeper spiritual enlightenment described by the writer of Hebrews when he exhorted Christians to "recall the former days in which, after you were *illuminated* (italics mine), you endured a great struggle with sufferings" (Heb. 10:32). The light of Jesus entering the world as Messiah is certainly more than the general revelation seen in the fine handiwork of God in the Creation. Jesus's light shines through the special revelation of God through His spoken and written words, as well as through His actions. As the Psalmist declared, "Your word is a lamp to my feet and a light to my path" (Ps. 119:105).

Until this illumination is internalized, it is a *knowing about* rather than an *abiding in* form of enlightenment. The first kind of illumination offers evidence that God exists. The second illumination may lead to the salvation of my soul, but not necessarily.

Many people have witnessed the intricate and complex wonders of living things and concluded, "Isn't evolution amazing!" Astronomers have observed the innumerable magnitude of stars in the heavens and studied the great order of constellations, paying homage to founders of the Big Bang theory. They would much rather credit a "black hole" origin of the universe than assent to a divine "First Mover" who brought the world into existence by His words. Likewise, many people have read the Bible firsthand, yet they shout the atheist's mantra: "There is no God!" Still other Bible readers have claimed ignorance, neither affirming nor denying the existence of a personal Deity. What does this suggest about the purpose and function of the Holy Spirit?

According to Bromily, being enlightened (*phōtízō*), as translated in Hebrews and Ephesians, "refers to the knowledge of the truth."[5] In this context, we must concede that Satan himself, who is called Lucifer (Isa.14:12), literally meaning "day star," was enlightened. He knows the truth, but he certainly does not have the indwelling of the Holy Spirit.

Accordingly, we must be very cautious about what we mean by "enlightenment." Other ungodly characters of the Bible were also enlightened in the same sense. Consider the first recorded account of the Holy Spirit given in Genesis 1:2 where we are told how "The Spirit of God was hovering over the face of the waters." He was there "when the earth was without form, and void." We are given no reference to the Spirit's action or involvement in the Creation, but in verse 3 we read, "Then God said, 'Let there be light'; and there was light." Could this have been Holy Spirit illumination? We are told nothing further about the Spirit of God until the Pharaoh of Egypt, whose dreams were interpreted by Joseph, asked, "Can we find such a one as this, a man in whom is the Spirit of God?" (Gen. 41:38). Of course, this is Pharaoh's interpretation and he knew nothing of the Holy Spirit as part of the triune God. But this knowledge possessed by Joseph indeed may have been the illuminating work of the Holy Spirit. We are not certain of this, since Joseph declares only that "God will give Pharaoh an answer of peace" to his dream (Gen. 41:16). Joseph never claimed to have any specific Holy Spirit illumination.

We later read in Exodus 31:3 that God equipped the craftsman Bezalel to construct the tabernacle, stating to Moses, "I have filled him with the Spirit of God, in wisdom, in understanding, in knowledge, and in all manner of workmanship." In Numbers 11:26 seventy elders of the Israelites prophesied when "the Spirit rested upon them." This also happened to Balaam (Num. 24:2) and to some of the judges of Israel (cf. Judges 3:10; 6:34), as well as numerous prophets of God.

In the New Testament, Jesus sent his twelve apostles to spread the news that "The kingdom of heaven is at hand," instructing them not to worry about how or what they would say, "for it is not you who speak, but the Spirit of your Father who speaks in you" (Matt. 10:7, 20). This Holy Spirit derived protection of words, both written and spoken, was a special gift of the Holy Spirit conferred upon the apostles and other authors of holy writ so that what was conveyed was exactly in line with God's will. This is the Bible definition of inspiration.

The apostle Paul speaks of this protection in the second chapter of First Corinthians when he asserts his (and the other apostles') authority. "Now we have received, not the spirit of the world, but the Spirit who is from God, that we might know the things that have been freely given to us by God. These things we also speak, not in words which man's wisdom teaches but which the Holy Spirit teaches, comparing spiritual things with spiritual." (vv. 12-13). Paul then further claims his authority to appraise the validity of all questionable doctrines but negates that anyone without inspiration should question his teaching (v. 15). He drives this point home by asking, "For who has known the mind of the Lord, that he should instruct Him? But we have the mind of Christ" (v. 16). Paul's use of the word "we" refers to the apostles, not to all Christians. When he claims to have the mind of Christ, he affirms that he is speaking by the authority of God.

This protection of words ended with the apostolic age, and we have no need of it any longer since we now have the authenticated word of God in its final form. The completion of the Scriptures has other implications that will be discussed further in the next chapter, as we apply actual rules of interpretation.

What is important to understand is that no interpreter of Scripture beyond the apostolic age has the gift of inspiration, which was bestowed exclusively to the Bible authors. No person innately has a full understanding of all that the Bible says. However, the Holy Spirit's gift of inspiration to those authors is one of the most precious gifts He has given to each of us today. This point is crucial to an understanding of how we approach the Bible as students of God's word. Again, we must keep in mind that God's way of doing things is not our way. God chose, in His infinite wisdom, to give us knowledge of Him through words written in human language. These words were given to us by divine inspiration.

The effects of this gift are dependent upon a sequence of events. We must first hear the words; then the words must be assimilated and understood. Finally, our response to these words will determine our eternal destiny. Before they can have their intended work in us, they must first be heard. If the words are distorted, misunderstood or misinterpreted in any way, the message may be compromised or changed, perhaps severely so. For this reason, sound interpretation of Scripture always must be the highest priority for all Christians. None of us shall ever be perfect in assigning meaning to these divine words, but a strong commitment to accurately teaching and understanding the message of salvation, holy living, and other doctrinal issues, will protect our own hearts and souls. It will also lead to a unified body of Christ.

If we insist on using the term "illumination" in the context of biblical interpretation, it should be used in the same sense as Paul's prayer for the Colossian brotherhood when he asked in his prayer, "that you may be filled with the knowledge of His will in all wisdom and spiritual understanding; that you may walk worthy of the Lord, fully pleasing Him, being fruit in every good work and increasing in the knowledge of God; strengthened with all might, according to His glorious power, for all patience and longsuffering with joy; giving thanks to the Father who has qualified us to be partakers of the inheritance of the saints in the light" (Col. 1: 9-12). Now *that* is Holy Spirit enlightenment!

This pursuit of holiness is a very distinct act from simply understanding what a Bible passage says. When Jesus appeared to His disciples, "He opened their understanding, that they might comprehend the Scriptures" (Luke 24: 45). Jesus here was acting as an interpreter. After this hermeneutical lesson, He then assured them that more was to come: "Behold, I send the Promise of My Father upon you" (Luke 24:49). This was the promise of the Holy Spirit whom Jesus called "another Helper" (John 14:16).

Endnotes

[1] Gerhard Maier, *"Biblical Hermeneutics,"* Crossway Books, Wheaton, 1994, p. 62.

[2] Roger R. Chambers, "Christianity and the Cults," *The Seminary Review* XXVII, December, 1981: 133-65

[3] Jack Cottrell, *The Holy Spirit: A Biblical Study*, College Press, Joplin, 2006, pp. 27-28.

[4] Ibid., p. 29.

[5] Geoffrey W. Bromiley, "Enlightened," *International Standard Bible Encyclopedia*, Vol. 2, Revised Ed., Eerdmans, Grand Rapids, 1982, p. 103.

Chapter 8

Common Errors in Interpretation

I magine a hypothetical situation designed to brew a perfect theological storm. Picture an auditorium full of new seminary graduates from all over the country who are gathered for a symposium on eschatology—the study of the end times. Presumably all graduates have likely completed at least one course in hermeneutics, thus having more than a rudimentary grasp on the rules of interpretation. Each scholar will be allowed podium time to defend his or her beliefs about how God will consummate the history of mankind.

Let me pause to point out that few Christians would consider their eschatological predilections to be a test of fellowship. However, neither are they likely to submit to a blank slate interpretation about what the Bible really says about this subject because the stakes are too high. If any cracks in the armor are acknowledged, it might demand a reconfiguring of their entire theology. So then, what would we expect to hear and see at such a gathering?

Most likely we would hear one scholar after another make all sorts of doctrinal claims that are diametrically opposed to each other. Every scholar would seek to defend their position, manipulating Scripture to justify their denomination's position on the grand finale. In no time at all, one scholar after another would advertise his or her understanding of what will happen in the course of time leading up to the final chapter of human history, and pure mayhem would break out. Voices would be raised. Snickering and muffled comments would be heard. Arms would be crossed in protest. Many would be flipping through pages of Scripture to prepare their skillful rebuttals against what they feel are the less enlightened scholars. Others would probably leave the auditorium in total exasperation. How would you react?

A neutral observer in this convention—if we may allow the hypothetical possibility of such a person—who understood the Scriptures might well observe many errors in scholarly thinking and in unbecoming behaviors. What if Jesus Himself were the observer? We can only speculate on what He might say, but such speculation might be worthwhile if it can teach us to guard against the things we all tend to do when feeling threatened in our beliefs. What common errors might we make in our search to know and understand God's plan to close the curtains? How certain can we be in our own claim to know how God will end the last chapter of human history? Or to know how He is acting in our lives at this time? The fact is, Christians are very divided on a great many issues, but this division most often arises from a failure to rationally and wholeheartedly search out what Scripture really has to say on these topics of contention, putting aside all of our stuffy pride and biases. The result of our blind pursuits is a cascade of errors that should never be allowed in the first place—like the pilot who crashed his plane. But the errors must first be recognized for what they are. If we can at least bring such potential errors to light, perhaps we shall be more able to guard against them in our own pursuit of truth. We must forever reject these blunders of the heart and mind in favor of a sincere yearning for a solid and true understanding of what God really meant to say in His spoken word. When we read the Bible, we must recognize and protect ourselves from the common mistakes that distort our understanding of God's decrees, so we may proclaim the truth in love without any compromise. In doing so, we promote true unity of the body of Christ.

I make no attempt here to create an exclusive list of errors in Bible interpretation, but here are a few common but serious problems that may incite us to unnecessarily draw spiritual battle lines against one another. Each error is briefly described, and an example or two is given in the course of discussion for clarification and to shed light on how we often fail to rightly divide God's word. Keep in mind that we are all capable of error, and these obstacles to unity are inherently the tools of Satan to promote discord in our Christian brotherhood. Hopefully, this will help us clean out our theological toolbox and use the right tools for the job.

1. Disregard for the absolute authority of Scripture

If the Bible is of divine origin, as it clearly claims to be, then it is without error, specifically in its original autographs. Simply put, no mistakes exist in God's written revelation to us. Hard sayings do exist. Symbolic language is present in some texts. And we certainly have some loose modern translations of the Bible that may possibly distort the meaning of the authors. However, in its original writings, there were no mistakes. Where possible errors may exist in the most dated manuscripts hitherto discovered, none of those errors in any way obscures God's truth in the way of salvation, or in any other essential teaching.

Unless we defend the biblical claim that the Bible is the God-breathed word (2 Timothy 3:16) that contains no errors in the original writings, we have no basis for proceeding further in the pursuit of knowing God and doing what God tells us to do. Any flippancy regarding the supremacy of Scripture in the governing of man's heart and soul is a blatant advertisement of one's ignorance of God. Any person who rejects the authority of Scripture has no chance of a deep and true fellowship with Christ. He who disdains the word of God is an imposter, whoever he may be. We must respect the veracity and power of God's message in order to appropriately respond to it. The alcoholic may be motivated to stop drinking not only because the Bible calls drunkenness debauchery and sin, but because he respects (fears) the judgment of his rebellion, and he chooses to honor God. But the drunkard who does not accept this biblical teaching has much less incentive to quit. The Christian's motivation to live a holy life derives from a belief that they are forgiven and free from the shackles of their former enslavement to sin. If God's word is pure and true, then we must respect it—all of it—and not elevate one teaching above another, or selectively ignore any passage on a whim because it does not suit our condition or perceived need. The Bible must be respected as the authoritative oracles of God, written for our good, and requiring due discernment in correct interpretation and application.

2. Manmade traditions that contradict Scripture

Tradition plays a strong role in all our lives. It gives us stability and makes life predictable. Expectations for social norms, religious beliefs, and family roles are clearly defined in every healthy society. In general, traditions are good. Coming home for the holidays is a tradition that unites families that live apart. The conveyance of customs or beliefs from one generation to another ensures that our heritage is not forgotten. A good tradition helps solidify strong values.

For this reason, the apostle Paul exhorted the Thessalonians to "stand fast and hold the traditions which you were taught, whether by word or our epistle" (2 Thess. 2:15). Thus, traditions can be a good thing. Traditions only become a problem when they conflict with the clear teaching of Scripture. Paul's former zeal for his Jewish traditions resulted in the persecution of many Christians. He was forced to forsake all the wrongful traditions of the Jewish sect after he began preaching the gospel. So must we do when our own traditions conflict with the teachings of the Christian Way.

Jesus challenged the Pharisees and scribes who accused Him of transgressing the tradition of the Jewish elders by asking them, "And why do you yourselves transgress the commandment of God for the sake of your tradition?" (Matt. 15:1-3). We shall never fully understand the truth of God's word so long as we are unwilling to put aside our contradictory and destructive traditions that blind us from seeing the plain truths of what Scripture clearly teaches. Allegiance to God should far supersede our adherence to all conflicting manmade sources of beliefs and principles.

In order for tradition to be put aside, it must be recognized for what it is, particularly when it is in direct conflict with God's word. Unfortunately, a great many traditions are held sacred because they are falsely believed to originate from biblical writings. Nowhere is this fact more revealed than in the traditions of Roman Catholicism. Having been raised in the Roman Catholic tradition, I experienced firsthand the power of the papacy and episcopate. My family ate fish on Fridays. We ate nothing before taking communion each Sunday morning. We regularly confessed our sins to a priest. We dutifully observed all "holy days of obligation" that included the Feast of Mary, the Mother of God and the Assumption of Mary into heaven. I ignorantly called the priest of our local parish "Father," being oblivious to the words of Matthew 23:9 ("Do not call anyone on earth your father; for One is your Father, He who is in heaven"). Biblical illiteracy creates a serious impediment to the extirpation of ungodly religious traditions, and our quest for unity as a Christian brotherhood. Some confessing Christians innocently defend their traditions with all fervor, fully believing them to be God ordained, not knowing they have no origin in Scripture. Willful ignorance is indefensible when God has plainly revealed His truth to us. We must always guard ourselves against an unrepentant spirit that darkens our understanding because of a blindness of the heart.

The celebration of Christmas is an example of an unbiblical mandate. Each December I have observed signs posted in the yards of well-meaning Christians that exhort us to keep Christ in Christmas. But nowhere in Scripture are we told to celebrate Jesus's birthday, and we are quite certain that Jesus was not born in December. The fact is, we have no biblical injunction to celebrate the Christmas holiday or the birth of our Savior. It may be a nice tradition, but Christians need not feel guilty for not recognizing this manmade holiday.

Some people enjoy the festivities, but others are heavy laden with the financial burden that goes along with buying presents to place under a Christmas tree. Others may feel guilty for not being able to afford any gifts. For many Christians and non-Christians alike, the Christmas season creates overwhelming stress and depression. The original spiritual intent of Christmas, if ever there was such a purpose, has been largely superseded by commercialism. Given its alleged pagan origin and the emotional trauma often associated with Christmas, each must decide for oneself its merits. The celebration of Christmas certainly should not be a test of fellowship.

The common error of exalting man-made traditions over Scripture, regardless of their source of origin or their perceived benefits or harms, can be avoided by having some knowledge of what the Bible actually says. Apart from knowing Scripture, we are no more equipped to navigate the waters of spiritual discernment than a ship without sails in a turbulent sea. Tradition must never preempt Scripture.

3. False assumptions based on prior false information

If someone was taught in childhood that communication with the dead is possible because Aunt Lucy had a OUIJA board and claimed to be able to call up the dead at will, he might assume that communication with the dead is a real possibility. If he later picks up a Bible and reads the account of the witch at Endor (1 Samuel 28:3-19) whom King Saul consorted with to call up Samuel from the dead, this person might naturally assume that this is the norm. This false assumption, based on prior misguided experience or teaching, could yield serious consequences in his spiritual development. Most of us have picked up some bad information along the way. Things that we may assume are Bible-based facts may be pure myth. And some things we consider myth may actually be true. Can you think of some teachings you once believed, only to shift gears as you spiritually matured? I suspect that hundreds of conflicting doctrinal issues could be discussed, such as perseverance of the saints (once saved, always saved), the proper mode of baptism, the process of sanctification, Holy Spirit regeneration, the nature of heaven and hell, and even the way of salvation. Some beliefs may be considered inconsequential in the big scheme of God's plan, while others may impact the way we live our daily Christian lives. Nevertheless, we would be wise to concede that small errors in our understanding of the Bible may lead to greater errors, and no misguided teaching is completely insignificant since each is a potential obstacle to unity.

Christians may also cling to false assumptions for the sake of convenience. How often have we justified our actions and beliefs simply because we have no real interest in knowing what the Bible truly says about choices we have made? Such knowledge may spoil our party and call for an undesired change in our thinking or behavior.

One example that hits home for many of us is our actual call to discipleship. We half-heartedly ask to know God's will. We seek specific, detailed and customized instructions telepathically transmitted into our brains, knowing full well that this sort of instruction would rob us of our free will. But ought we to know the will of God? Yes! It is written: "For this is the will of God, your sanctification:

that you abstain from sexual immorality; that each of you should know how to possess his own vessel in sanctification and honor." (1 Thess. 4:3-4).

Now this clearly stated will of God flies in the face of many churches today. In our new era of enlightenment that not only tolerates sexual immorality but actually embraces it, some churches would argue that such a sin no longer exists. The consequence of such rebellion is fearful. In the same breath we are told, "he who rejects this does not reject man, but God, who has also given us His Holy Spirit" (1 Thess. 4:8).

These willful oversights of the clear and straightforward commandments of God cannot really be called false assumptions. They are nothing less than acts of defiance that destroy all hope of a unified church body. If there be any false assumptions in these cases, it is in the assumption that God will forgive their voluntary ignorance. The good interpreter must strive to eliminate all volitional ignorance. The entirety of the Bible must be read and properly regarded, and no doctrine should be conveniently swept under the carpet if we are to contend for a composite unity of God's people based on all His precepts.

4. Ignorance of Bible history, geography and ancient customs

Both the Old and New Testament are replete with references to places, customs and traditions that were common knowledge when the Bible authors penned their words. Such geographic locations as Gehenna, Valley of Hinnom and Megiddo were real places and were associated with real events. When such places came to be associated with hell and the "battle of Armageddon," the association was much clearer and relevant to the ancient denizens living in or near these localities. Thousands of years later, the meanings of geographic references have been blurred to the point of obscurity, unless we study the history of that era and culture.

When the apostle Peter exhorted us, "gird your minds for action," we cannot fully grasp its meaning unless we understand the practice of "girding the loins," which was common jargon in the first century AD. Reading the Bible without understanding the history of past civilizations is like a professional musician trying to read a medical journal. Without a background in medicine, he will miss the meaning of much information. The fact is, we can never grasp the full meaning of any verse of Scripture that contains colloquialisms without having studied the culture, and in particular, its anachronistic vernacular. But as we grasp the meaning of ancient dialects, we are more deeply moved by the import of symbols and idiosyncratic words associated with this foreign speak. Reference works such as *Eerdmans Handbook to the Bible*[1] and *The New Unger's Bible Dictionary*[2] are most helpful in this pursuit. In the present day, we have innumerable Bible reference works that are most helpful in better understanding foreign and ancient cultures. The reader is left to explore and utilize these resources to open the magnificent treasures found in Scripture.

5. Sensitive topics such has homosexuality, suicide, finances, and politics

Let's face it, some topics dealing with current affairs and new social norms are difficult to discuss simply because we do not wish to offend—or we are afraid of being attacked. Or perhaps we do not know how to broach an emotional topic without fear of misunderstanding or reprisal. At a time when even the medical community is being strong-armed into accepting as normal such perversions as transgenderism and gender fluidity, espousing one's opposing faith convictions could easily result in termination of employment, a lawsuit, and possibly even jail time. Many Christians have family members or friends who are homosexual or who have opposing political views on these heated issues. When such views contradict Scripture, the boldness needed to lovingly confront this sin in the church often flees rapidly, even in church leaders. In this arena, the cost of discipleship may become physically palpable, painful and costly.

When it comes to finances, we are sometimes sensitized by our own personal state of affairs. What successful businessman wishes to be reminded of the deceitfulness of riches? And how do we approach the subject of the vast array of modern snares that are not directly addressed in the Scripture? That the Bible is silent about the potential harms of social media doesn't mean that we have liberty to ignore the evils present in this popular commodity of contemporary life.

We are called to "hold fast what is good. Abstain from every form of evil" (1 Thess. 5:21-22). Unfortunately, this cannot be done without offending some, however humble our rejection of evil. In some circumstances, we *should* be silent because we do not know all the circumstances leading up to an act or event that we consider to be repulsive. How often have we heard of the "selfish act" of the person who committed suicide? I'm not sure that the desperate mindset of an ill-fated person contemplating suicide is capable of being selfish. Having come face-to-face with such tragedies during my years as a physician, I can recall several suicides that were committed out of sheer emotional or physical agony.

All humans seek relief from pain. Suicide should never be condoned, but neither are we in a position to judge the suicide victim's motives. Many Christians maintain that suicide is a damning offense against God, but errors of interpretation may lead to such a conclusion.

I recall, years ago in residency, treating an AIDS patient who readily confided in me that he actually hated being homosexual. He had been sexually abused in every way, and he had no idea of how to change the lifestyle that was forced on him throughout his entire childhood. He expressed to me a longing to have a healthy marriage and to raise children, but he had no idea how to create a normal lifestyle that most people take for granted. On one occasion he delighted in seeing my family together as a wholesome unit. He longed for it, but the concept of a healthy heterosexual relationship was as foreign to him as a homosexual relationship is to me.

Does that make me a homophobe? Certainly not! Should I have justified his lifestyle due to his circumstances? No. Situation ethics doctrine is nothing more than a justification for sin. I truly can understand the mind this victim of abuse. I do intellectually grasp the reason for his lifestyle, but I must never condone it because God does not condone it. The sin of homosexuality is no more or less a sin than any other sin defined in Scripture. The Bible clearly teaches that homosexuality is an abomination. But so are lying, cheating, stealing, rudeness, pride, selfishness, insensitivity, greed and wrongful anger. I am just as guilty before God as he is. His sins are no darker than mine. How then do we respond to such people, such situations?

First, we must always guard our tongues when voicing opinions about emotionally charged events or topics. As James tells us, "Mercy triumphs over judgment" (Jas. 2:13). The tongue is best controlled by always questioning our motive when we feel compelled to verbally expose ungodly behavior, to cast the first stone. But we must never be afraid to call a sinful act exactly what it is, based on what the Scripture teaches. If such people (including ourselves) are ever to be led out of a sinful lifestyle, the remedy begins with the healing power of Christ. What sinners need to see are kindness, a merciful regard, a good word, and a helping hand. We were given the Ten Commandments to reveal in cold, hard stone that we have all disobeyed each of God's commandments, in view of what the New Testament reveals.

Humbling as it may be, I must confess that I have sinned. I must never justify my sin or call it by another name. Sin is a rebellious act against God. To deny my sin is to negate the authority of Scripture. It would be the clay disavowing the potter. The best way to approach all sensitive topics and confrontations with sin is to model the Master. We should receive the sinner with sensitivity, compassion and love, but at the same time offer the remedy for all sin. We must also preserve our own souls and not be turned like a weathervane to declare evil good. With righteous but humble indignation, we must expose sin when the Bible declares an act sinful. As the apostle Paul writes, "Have no fellowship with the unfruitful works of darkness, but rather expose them" (Eph. 5:11).

Three scenarios may present themselves when confronting sin. The first is the sinner who does not know Christ as his Savior. In God's righteous decree, he is without excuse and shall face certain judgment unless he repents. But the unregenerate sinner can be expected to act no other way. The natural man behaves carnally. He must be told and shown the better way.

Another situation entails a stumbling brother or sister in Christ. We should offer a loving hand rather than cast a stone. With a good word from Scripture, never forgetting our own weakness and propensity to sin, we must gently declare the righteous way set forth by God alone, showing mercy with the hope of bringing forth repentance. The apostle Paul advised his fellows, "Brethren, if a man is overtaken in any trespass, you who are spiritual restore such a one in a spirit of gentleness, considering yourself lest you also be tempted" (Gal. 6:1). We must show the better way in all its glory and strive to practice it as we exhort others to do the same. Jesus never condoned the sin or the sinner. Instead, He was always full of mercy to the repentant sinner, declaring, "Go and sin no more" (John 8:11).

A third case may result from a self-seeking leadership that causes others to stumble and lead them astray. Here is where Jesus showed little patience, and He never failed to expose the sin of prideful defiance. His contempt for pious self-righteousness, false teachers and hypocrites was unrestrained. Jesus held nothing back as he condemned the Pharisees (See Matt. 23: 13-36). Surely Jesus would have similar choice words for the modern profiteers and false teachers of our day. Neither should we tolerate anyone who willfully perverts the word of God, leading to the destruction of blind sheep.

6. Cultic biases of denominations

The esoteric affirmations that serve to brand each herd of Christianity apart from all others are a major stumbling block, if not *the single greatest obstacle*, to Christian unity. Sadly, few followers of Christ are even aware of all the nuances in their denomination's beliefs, and how their sect differs from all others. Fewer still understand what the Bible really says in its entirety about any of the unique doctrinal biases preached so avidly from the pulpit.

A sort of brainwashing takes place in each denomination, and members are expected to think and speak alike regarding these partisan preferences. Any challenges to these endearing beliefs are regarded as spurious errors in need of correction. Doctrinal "deviants" are not well tolerated, and they are pressured to blindly conform to the carefully defined creed. In this way, the purity of the sectarian pedigree is ensured. Better to cull a few dissenters at the outset than to allow any serious questioning of established ways. Seldom are we willing to look ourselves squarely in the mirror to ask if we truly should stake full claim to all that our sectarian creeds avow, without understanding if these dogmas are really in accord with scriptural teaching. We seem wholly oblivious to the harm of such compromise in our quest for truth and spiritual formation. God did not create us to be dim-witted automatons. We must always reference the holy Book to test all proclamations made, regardless of the source.

The reader here is forewarned. I am all too aware that a threat against any of our denominational dogmas is likely to be received about as well as a tag from a 300-million Volt stun gun. Challenging another's religious conviction may quickly expose the fangs of an otherwise docile servant of Christ like no other offense. A treasured belief by one brother challenged by a believer of a different Christian sect is likely to elicit a reaction much like a grizzly bear protecting her cubs from potential harm. You are apt to expose ugly behavior in a Christian brother by challenging any of his landmark beliefs. Such behavior has manifested itself particularly among some of the most renowned scholars of our time, for they have much invested in their claims.

Of course, human nature being what it is, I can understand the animosity. Their reputations are at stake. Admitting a mistake is humbling and rubs hard against thin skin. Scholars are revered within their denominations and considered pillars of the faith. People look to them for direction, so exposing flaws in their thinking cuts deeply. I must confess that I have experienced a bristling myself when my fondly held beliefs have been challenged on multiple occasions. But I am the better Christian for it. Since this is such a sensitive topic for all of us, I will do my best to tread lightly as we dig a little deeper.

Leaders of religious denominations, of necessity, seek to regulate our behavior and thinking. Remember that a denomination, by definition, is a religious organization having its own distinctive beliefs that set it apart from other Christian faith groups. A denomination is a division in the body of Christ. The dictum of each denomination in essence states this: we are different from you. While most Christian denominations would acknowledge others as a legitimate part of the body of Christ, this allowance is predicated on the tacit notion that God will make allowances for the less informed or errant brotherhood of other denominations. The Calvinist would figuratively consider the Arminian to be among the outer circle of Christ's followers, as would the Arminian the Calvinist.

Some specific requirements of a given church persuasion are virtually a test of brotherhood, while others are acknowledged to be of lesser significance. Other softer decrees might be regarded merely as a measure of spiritual maturity or even the degree of biblical understanding that one has achieved. The extent to which one conforms to and espouses the party line determines their standing in the brotherhood.

The ruling principle is, if you want to be accepted by us, think as we do and say as we say. If the espoused teachings are in accord with sound Scriptural teaching, this is a good thing. If not, then you are being misguided at best, or deluded in cultic fashion at worst. The Christian standard ought always to be upheld. Promoting good behavior, setting boundaries and expectations for holy living and corporate worship are essential. The Bible speaks of this at length, but sometimes denominationalists take strong issue over matters deemed of lesser importance by God. They litigate the way we dress, how we should speak, and what we should believe about this or that, with whom we can and cannot fellowship, and how we must fellowship, in contrast to what the Bible actually instructs. This is damaging to the Christian body.

When the goal of maintaining the integrity of a sect's core beliefs usurps the authority of God's word, a serious problem exists. Such mandates as avoiding certain foods, worshipping on the correct day, allowing or disallowing certain or all musical instruments, women wearing only dresses and no jewelry, manifesting or not manifesting certain spiritual gifts, men dressing likewise in appropriate attire—this becomes the status quo and delineates the right form of "godliness." Such biblically unprecedented worship and lifestyle idiosyncrasies, misuses of spiritual gifts, and following specific modern-day "prophets" seriously stunt our spiritual growth. Violations of these skewed teachings may cause some to be ostracized from the church group, regardless of their Bible-based convictions. This is cultic.

Under such circumstances, a choice must be made; follow the iconic norms or obey the impregnable teachings of Scripture. Once "in the family" of a radical sect, the decision to comply or depart is never easy. The need to belong tugs heavily at our heartstrings. How far are we willing to go in our need to conform, to fit in, to belong? Devout allegiance to unscriptural teachings is dangerous and foolish, threatening our eternal fate. If we must harbor biases, let them accurately and completely coincide with the biases of Jesus, such as showing no partiality, avoiding oppression of the poor, and pursuing things that build one another's true spiritual character according to a bona fide biblical model. Let our biases echo what that Bible proclaims, nothing more, nothing less.

Have you ever questioned any teaching or preaching in your local church that seemed to contradict Scripture? If so, what response did you receive? If the inquiry was not pondered in a Berean spirit, and the answer was not given in a straightforward manner, then you may have cause for concern. Remember the biblical command to "test all things" (I Thess. 5:21). Remember also that every teaching that departs from the Scripture is of no little consequence and may even jeopardize your soul. Pay attention to what the Bible says, and always approach it with an open mind to see if what you are taught agrees with God's teaching. Confronting untruths takes great courage, but if done in a spirit of genuineness and humility, it shall bear good fruit. As you contend for the faith once given for all, you will become a strong ambassador for Christ and a faithful advocate for Christian unity. You will glorify the Holy Spirit by honoring and respecting His great work of inspiration.

7. Neglecting the elementary principles of human language

Not everyone has a solid grasp of their native tongue, but some rudimentary understanding of language is necessary to survive in the world. Very few of us understand the Hebrew, Aramaic, or Greek dialects. Fewer still have good training in grammar, syntax (sentence structure) and lexicology (study of words), regardless of what language we may be reading or speaking.

Consequently, many Christians are somewhat handicapped when it comes to reading even an English version of the Bible. Sincere Bible believers make an abundance of interpretive errors because they cannot or will not follow the basic rules of human language. Add to this a biased teacher with an agenda, and spiritual chaos follows. Without a rudimentary command of the rules of human language, and without the discipline to follow said rules by those capable of doing so, we have no chance of accurately understanding Scripture. Until we accept the truth that the Holy Spirit protected the *words written in human language*, we shall never be able to rightly honor the Spirit in His powerful revelatory work of God's will for us.

What does this mean? If we cannot or will not properly assimilate words and sentences constructed by means of the common rules that make communication possible, we are doomed to misunderstand the meaning of all written communication. To some, this assertion may sound like a pathetic statement of the obvious, but let's analyze the problem. First of all, we must comprehend the simple but critical fact that the rules necessary to understanding all human languages and are not subject to arbitration. Rules are standardized and yield a predictable outcome. These principles are immutable. If the rules of grammar were debatable or whimsical, then human communication would be impossible. Anyone who has ever read a novel, a poem, or a historical document with understanding, derives comprehension from the rules of language being followed such that the writer has a means of transferring information to the reader. If either the reader or the writer ignores the rules of language, meaningful communication is impossible, and understanding of the information is compromised.

In the matter of interpreting and understanding the Scriptures, the same principle is true. The Holy Spirit, being divine, cannot err in communicating the written revelation of God. As Jesus claimed, "the Scripture cannot be broken" (John 10:35). God gave man an innate capacity to communicate through a form of language shared by no other animal. Human language consists primarily of verbal and written communication. Man is also bestowed with a wide array of facial expressions and gestures far exceeding that of any other mammal. Moreover, man alone among all creatures in the animal kingdom has the capacity to contemplate both past and future experiences.

Another solely human attribute is man's power to contemplate eternity (Ecc. 3:11). Man is uniquely equipped to respond to God's written communication. These special human traits allow us to hear, analyze, comprehend, and respond to the word of God. The rules of grammar pertain as much to the Bible as they do to any other book. We can read and enjoy a good novel and comprehend instructions on how to repair an automobile. We can learn about the natural universe by studying scientific textbooks. We are able to digest a detailed account of history and make sense of wise proverbs. The emotions of our hearts are triggered by beautiful poetry.

As young children we learned the alphabet to make words. Then we were taught how to put words together in a meaningful way. In a short time, toddlers and young children learn to apply the rules of language so they can read nursery rhymes and fairytales. As they continue their mastery of language, new worlds open up to them and new possibilities are discovered.

The Bible is similarly discovered through these principles of written communication. God created our brains for such interaction, and for this reason God has given us a written record of His nature, His plan for mankind, and His will—all in human language. How do I know Jesus loves me? "The Bible tells me so."

But if the common principles of human discourse are ignored then the content of the message is compromised. For some reason, many well-meaning but ill-guided Christians ascribe to the Bible a unique classification that somehow allows for, or even demands, the abrogation of these precepts of written language. Simply stated, this leads to false doctrine and gross misunderstandings of God's revelation to us. Never is an alleged justification for suspending the rules of human language valid. When we fail to apply the structural rules of proper grammar, syntax, morphology, semantics and lexicography, we pervert God's message and suffer the consequences of this dereliction, not the least being discord and confusion in the body of Christ. We simply cannot ignore the elementary principles of human language if we wish to honor the inspirational work of the Holy Spirit.

8. Reading beyond what is written

This flaw is a most pernicious seed of division among the family of God. The error needs little explanation. Anyone who has sat through a Bible study has likely witnessed the distortion of a Bible passage by someone making a false inference, or by subjectively adding to or taking away from the Bible text.

A gross exaggeration of this would be a reader who claims that infidelity is acceptable because Jesus thwarted the killing of an adulteress by telling her accusers, "He who is without sin among you, let him throw a stone at her first" (John 8:7). Jesus did not condone what she had done; He merely taught a principle, namely that we are all guilty of transgressing God's laws.

The temptation to read beyond what is written is strong for a number of reasons. First, we may wish to apply a verse to an event in our own lives. We want to make the Scripture "fit" our situation. Another possible reason is guilt. We might seek to justify a sin, and therefore distort a clear teaching against that sin. We see this clearly within the lesbian-gay-bisexual-transgender (LGBT) movement. We also see it when telling little white lies, and whenever we knowingly violate civil laws such as the speed limit. Such distortion of biblical truth may serve a practical purpose for sinners here, but it will yield no benefit in the hereafter. Whenever we assume words or meaning beyond what is written, whether by subtraction or by addition, we pervert God's teaching. This is a grave offense.

9. Alleged conflicts between Scripture and science

A general precept to remember is that the Bible was written primarily to show us the way of salvation, giving us the means of knowing God through His own words. His primary purpose for writing to us is to reveal His plan of redemption, whereby we may respond to His offer of being united with Him for all eternity. Although not intended to be a science textbook, many references to the natural world and the laws of physics are made throughout the Bible. When God wrote to His human creation, He did not intend to confer upon us all scientific knowledge. (Where then would be the joy of new scientific discoveries?) This is not the purpose of Scripture.

References to the creation and science in the Bible are made in the common dialect of the time, using the current knowledge and understanding of the writers in their world. Nonetheless, we are given affirmations of some scientific facts, such as of the earth being round (Isaiah 40:22), but this information is secondary. The most awe-inspiring act of God's creation is elucidated when God confronts Job (Job 38-41). While the Bible is not a science textbook, we do have much supportive scientific evidence that renders the biblical creation view of the cosmos highly tenable.

The student who is indoctrinated in the theory of evolution at a secular or even a Christian school is often spiritually handicapped. Evolution is merely a theory that requires the same faith as, if not more faith than, is essential to believe the Genesis creation account. Evolution theory, however, is taught as fact in most public schools. The majority of young students unwittingly swallow evolution science hook, line, and sinker, never questioning its validity.

As these children become adults, they tend to regard the Genesis account of creation as fiction or mythology because they have already been programmed. Those who question evolution theory may fear retribution or humiliation. Oftentimes, Bible-educated adults feel compelled to deny the biblical teaching on God's creation, or to somehow attempt to blend the two by distorting the Bible record. They wish to save face in the secular world because they have been taught the "facts" of evolution, being duped into believing that no harmony of science and Scripture is possible. Secular opinion then becomes their standard for establishing any further religious truth, leading to many false assumptions when reading Scripture.

If the creation story cannot be trusted as valid and accurate, then where does this leave the rest of Scripture? Suddenly the Genesis record of a day may be arbitrarily understood to refer figuratively to a million or a billion years. We must appreciate the fact that prior false teachings are difficult to unravel and are ominous hindrances to an accurate understanding of the Bible. In the secular realm, modern science clearly eclipses the Bible on all matters concerning origins of life, but such "science" is often shoddy, biased and funded by those who are bewitched by an atheistic or agnostic faith. For those wishing to explore this topic in detail, see Morris's compelling treatise on the harmony of Scripture and science.[3]

Sometimes scientists cite technical inaccuracies in Scripture to bolster their positions. Such distorted arguments as the mustard seed not being the smallest of all seeds to discredit the Bible are absurd. The mustard seed was a very small seed that burgeons into a very large tree. That is the point of the illustration. It is compared to the growth of the kingdom of God. It is not a dissertation on the smallest seed in the plant kingdom; but it is most useful to the Judean hearer of the parable in understanding how God's kingdom shall grow. The mustard seed existed in their world, was the smallest of seeds in their world, and they could therefore relate to the object and the principle. (Read Mark 4: 30-32.) Never forget that the predictability in the universe allows for scientific discovery, rendering science a product of God's Creation.

10. Apparent contradictions

The Bible is often accused of being overtly contradictory in its content. For example, James tells us, "The effective prayer of a righteous man can accomplish much" (James 5:16), whereas Paul tells us in Romans 3:10 that "There is none righteous, no, not one." Are these statements contradictory? No. Taken in context, James is speaking of *relative* righteousness, i.e., of one who is earnestly seeking to live a holy life compared to a devout anarchist. Paul, on the other hand, is speaking of the sinful nature of man, who is unrighteous when compared alongside the perfect righteousness of God. This was the error Job made when he declared himself righteous. Compared to most, he was a cut above his peers, perhaps way above, with regard to his relative righteousness. But compared to the absolute righteousness of God, Job's righteous deeds "are like filthy rags" (Isa. 64:6). If we keep in mind that "all Scripture is inspired by God" (2 Tim. 3:16), then real contradictions cannot be present. Whenever we read something that seems to contradict another principle or truth, we must search deeper into Scripture to resolve the apparent contradictions.

Another example of an apparent contradiction is found in Luke 18:29-30 when Jesus told His disciples, "Assuredly, I say to you, there is no one who has left house or parents or brothers or wife or children, for the sake of the kingdom of God, who shall not receive many times more in this present time, and in the age to come eternal life." But the apostle Paul instructs, "If anyone does not provide for his own, and especially for those of his household, he has denied the faith, and is worse than an unbeliever" (1 Tim. 5:8).

At first glance, these two passages seem to be saying opposite things. Jesus was not telling his disciples to neglect their responsibilities to their family, he was explaining the importance of putting God first. He also was speaking to his twelve chosen followers who were in the most crucial mentorship of all times. When we make the mistake of ignoring the immediate purpose and meaning of a passage when comparing it to another, the error of apparent contradictions may thwart our genuine pursuit of truth.

ii. Hard sayings in Scripture

Even the best of scholars do not have a complete understanding of all Scripture. The apostle Peter points this out when he says some of Paul's writings contain "some things hard to understand" (2 Pet. 3:16). However, Peter's theme in his second letter is cautioning believers to beware of false teachers whose sole intent is to lead astray those of the true faith. He also points out that the hard sayings must be properly addressed and accurately interpreted; sayings "which untaught and unstable people twist to their own destruction, as they do also the rest of the Scriptures" (2 Pet. 3:16). Thus, the difficult things to understand in Scripture should serve to validate our personal limitations and frailty of mind when it comes to comprehending all that God reveals to us. As aforementioned, we live in a world far different from the ancient world. This barrier no doubt also lends to some difficulties in our comprehension. Whatever the obstacles to our understanding, we are better off saying nothing than to arbitrarily distort Scripture in such a way that could spiritually harm us. We are admonished to not argue over doubtful things (Rom. 14:1); and hard sayings, by their very nature, may raise doubts in our minds. F. F. Bruce has written an excellent work on hard sayings in the Bible.[4]

Before we declare any passage of Scripture a "hard saying," we must reach deep into our souls with all diligence and ask ourselves if a passage is truly hard to *understand* or just hard to *accept*. Many easy-to-understand biblical passages are hard to accept because of the reader's own cultural biases and preconceived norms, or perhaps because of personal sin.

Christian feminists struggle greatly with some of the apostle Paul's teaching on gender roles, not because the text is obscure or challenging to comprehend, but because it does not jive with their ungodly agenda. Feminists would read 1 Timothy 2:11-12 and declare this a hard saying since it assigns a duty of submissiveness to women in corporate worship. They would likely cite in their defense Galatians 3:28 which declares that males and females are all equal in the sight of God. In doing so, they expose their refusal to accept God's plan for the different roles of men and women in His wise design of mankind.

Yes, God is sexist! He created us males and females, each sex having strengths and weaknesses that render us suitable for various roles. These roles are complementary and have nothing to do with the intrinsic value of men and women, race, social status or any other social or cultural divides.

"There is neither Jew nor Greek, there is neither slave nor free man, there is neither male nor female; for you are all one in Christ Jesus," says Paul in Galatians 3:28. But this equality pertains to salvation and intrinsic value, as is evident by the preceding verse

(3:27) that declares, "For all of you who were baptized into Christ have clothed yourselves with Christ."

While we are all declared equal in God's estimation with regard to the value of our souls, God saw fit to assign roles to males and females by His creation design, and this point is evidenced beyond all doubt when Paul states elsewhere, "Let a woman learn in silence with all submission. And I do not permit a woman to teach or to have authority over a man, but to be in silence" (1 Timothy 2:11-12). This passage is not hard to understand, as Paul here plainly clarifies the role of women in public worship.

For some, though, Paul's statement is hard to accept. These verses apply for all time, beyond any doubt, because verse 13 states, "For Adam was formed first, then Eve." This appeal to the creation of mankind through Adam and Eve bears weight in showing that this was a gender role assigned to God from the beginning. If your blood is beginning to boil right now, it is only because you have been indoctrinated in the false teachings of the feminist movement, rendering this easy-to-comprehend passage difficult to accept.

In pointing this out, I do not intend to minimize the many marital and cultural abuses of women that led to the feminist movement. In fact, the Bible clearly renounces such treatment. The teachings of the Bible have overwhelmingly served the cause of women more than any other religion. When this same apostle wrote, "Husbands, love your wives, just as Christ also loved the church and gave Himself for her" (Eph. 5:25), we men must understand the depth of Paul's point. Christ died for the church. In other words, no sacrifice is too great for a husband to willingly make for his wife. That's a lot of love and devotion! If such a God-ordained love were to be practiced by all men, we would hear nothing of any feminist movement. For those wishing to better understand the controversies of feminism and a solid biblical exposition on this issue, read Jack Cottrell's definitive work on this subject.[5]

Given any situation, men and women think, act, reason, and behave differently. This is purely by God's design, and both sexes are blessed by the dissimilarities. Women have estrogen as their dominant sex hormone, and men have testosterone as theirs. Sex hormone dominance is genetically programmed at conception. (Therefore sex determination is not subject to debate, as we see with the gender fluidity movement.) If you were to look at the human brain of a male and female side by side, you would see a visible anatomical difference. The female tract between the two brain hemispheres (corpus callosum) is significantly larger compared to the male. Thus, women are said to have eyes in the back of their heads.

Women naturally multitask, whereas men tend to have a one-track mind. Men compartmentalize. Men are accused of having "selective hearing." Having more testosterone renders the male the physically stronger of the sexes because testosterone induces muscle hypertrophy (increase in size of the muscle fibers). Hence, the abuse of anabolic steroids. But testosterone also renders the male ego fragile. Women, if you really want to get a man to do something, appeal to his ego. Physical strength does not necessarily connote emotional strength. Every woman knows that a man suffering from the flu wants his mommy for comfort, never daddy. Many a soldier on the battlefield suffering from a mortal wound will cry out in his final moments for his mommy, not caring what the other burly men around him think. This is because estrogen renders the woman a natural nurturer.

The differences between the sexes are myriad, and are something to be celebrated as a magnificent product of God's creativity. Men and women complement each other. We need one another. The love between a man and a woman is beautiful to behold, and a godly marriage exemplifies the love between Christ and his church.

This example of an "easy" hard saying hopefully reveals how many verses of Scripture are only declared hard because of the hardness of our own hearts as we refuse to accept some very straightforward teachings from the inspired words of God. But some passages in the Bible are more difficult to understand, and these require much searching and careful discernment. One example of a truly "hard saying" follows right after Paul further clarifies the role of women in worship, in his first letter to Timothy. He first states, "And Adam was not deceived, but the woman being deceived, fell into transgression" (1 Tim. 2:14). This tells us something of the nature of a woman that renders her more susceptible to deceit. It is not at all an insult to woman, but it points perhaps to the more trusting nature of a woman. How many women are deceived by the craftiness of a salesman or auto mechanic, or by the insincere shrewdness of a selfish "lover"?

Now look at the next verse: "Nevertheless she will be saved in childbearing if they continue in faith, love, and holiness, with self-control" (1 Tim. 2:15). When I first read this verse many years ago, my first response was, huh? I had no idea why Paul wrote those words, and I frankly wished he hadn't written them. Years later, in the course of my obstetrics practice, I better understood the trials of a woman in labor, which could even, on very rare occasions, be life threatening. Even in the relatively easy deliveries, I may have lost some hearing from the painful cries elicited by women in active labor. (Okay, just kidding.) But what exactly did Paul mean to convey in this verse? I'll drop this question and leave it to you the interpreter to rightfully discern the meaning. This is a hard saying, with plausible answers to be discovered in the course of diligent study.

We have many good reference works and other books written to help us sort out the truly hard sayings of Scripture. But of utmost importance is our own discernment in what we consider to be a hard saying. We might first check our attitude and ask ourselves why we perceive a saying to be difficult. The religious leaders found many of Jesus's teachings hard to grasp. Once we eliminate our own biases and sinful tendencies as a cause for a hard saying, then we need only to investigate further.

12. Willful misrepresentation

Every generation in all societies has been plagued by shams and scams, and we encounter many of them in the religious world of our day. God pulls no punches when He speaks of the punishment awaiting those who have deceived those who might otherwise have come to the knowledge of truth. Imposters abound and are often popular commodities, but we are obliged to expose them (Eph. 5:11). In reality, many of them are found in the spotlights and draw large crowds. We often see them thriving financially, being well-supported monetarily by their many gullible followers. False teachers are manipulative deceivers with smooth tongues and inflated egos. They often don three-piece suits and have a penchant for seeking out vulnerable and weak believers. However, each of these false teachers had a beginning. These counterfeits may appear in the back door of our own local churches at any time. They portray themselves as angels of light, as messengers of God, as having special authority that commands obedience. Each has his angle to hook the spiritually weak. We must forever be aware of them, as they always leave behind them a tornado's wake of destruction. I am grateful for such warriors as Justin Peters whose efforts in exposing false teachers are likely saving many from deceit.[6] Great shall be his reward, and ours, as we contend for the faith!

Sometimes deception is blatantly obvious, but most of the time it is densely camouflaged. Misrepresentation of Scripture by theological serpents can be couched in flowery and smooth words that make it hard to detect, and this is not something exclusive to cultic or pseudo-Christian denominations. Any strong emotion deriving from some struggle in our past lives may lead us to willfully misrepresent God's teaching, regardless of church affiliation.

Consider, for example, the controversial subject of alcohol. In American society, we see the great harms of alcoholism all around us. Statistically, an alcoholic has a fifty percent chance of becoming and staying sober. The un-recovering alcoholic is very likely to drink himself into the grave. Teen pregnancy is often associated with alcohol and drug abuse. How many times has the intoxicated driver claimed victims on the road? A child raised by an alcoholic parent suffers much abuse. Any Christian victimized firsthand by the harmful effects of alcohol is likely to condemn it and claim that such "spirits" are purely demonic. The non-victims who have witnessed the sufferings of others may be fully sympathetic to their sentiments. But is the Christian to be condemned because he partakes of a glass of wine on occasion? Are we able to rightly claim that the Bible condemns all use of the fermented fruit of the vine?

Here we must be very careful to not misrepresent what Scripture actually teaches. While our motives may be genuine and sincere, we can easily and willfully misrepresent what the Bible teaches because of charged emotions. Willful misrepresentation may be understandable, but it is never excusable. Many conservative religious sects also claim that dancing is evil. But the Preacher of Ecclesiastes teaches us plainly that there is "a time to mourn, and a time to dance" (Eccles. 3:5).

Consider nuclear energy, opiates, sugar, television, social media, weapons, genetic medicine, and new inventions. All of these have the potential for good and evil. All either have been or shall be used to improve our quality of life and to destroy it. We could easily make a case against all of these, but we can also tout their benefits.

Nuclear energy is clean, but its force can cause mass casualties. Opioids have greatly lessened pain, but heroin abuse has killed many addicts. Processed sugar is tasty, but sugar addiction causes obesity that leads to diabetes, heart disease, high blood pressure, strokes and worn out joints. Think of how your perspective on each of these things is influenced by your current lifestyle. I could readily use Scripture to proof-text the position that God hates sugar, and so should we. Smart phones have revolutionized communication, but childhood suicide has become rampant due to social media bullying. When we arbitrarily decide something is good or bad for us, we might be right in our choosing for the sake of our own conscience. But when we impose the same decree on others, we become legalists who may wrongly judge a fellow heir in Christ. We are exhorted in Romans 14 to not dispute doubtful things (v. 1) and to be fully convinced in our own minds about these things (v. 5). Willful misrepresentation sometimes stems from a true conviction that is not aligned with actual biblical teaching, and this does nothing to edify. This is a serious error in interpretation.

13. Simple breakdown of logic

We may sometimes read, fully comprehend, and accept one passage of Scripture, and then unwittingly reject another passage that does not fit into our current belief system. We may even subconsciously reject sound doctrine because of a firm overriding conviction.

An eager young Christian convert was once severely scolded by a more mature brother upon hearing the neophyte eagerly declare, "I am now the light of the world!" The mature brother quickly corrected him by sharing with him the verse in John 8:12 in which Jesus declared, "I am the light of the world." The Christian newcomer looked puzzled as he recited his new memory verse, Matthew 5:14, "You are the light of the world." Who was correct?

Both appealed to a biblical truth-claim, and both are correct in their interpretation. Jesus did claim to be the light of the world, but He also declared to His disciples that they were the light of the world. Then He went on to explain how we should let our light shine (Matt. 5:16). Having not mastered the Scripture, the more mature Christian wished to reverently defend Jesus's supremacy as the light of the world, but he offended a new convert when he ignorantly assumed a disciple could not also be a light. We see then that ignorance of Scripture may lead to illogical conclusions. The mature brother errantly reasoned, if Jesus is the light of the world, then you are *not* the light of the world. This is a false conclusion based on Jesus's own words that declare "you" (followers of Christ) to also be the light of the world.

The "you" must be properly assigned, of course, for correct interpretation. Logic would also clearly suggest that the light of Jesus would be the brighter light. The light of Jesus is intrinsic; He is the very source of light. A Christian's light is reflected. Therefore, a Christian's light cannot be brighter than Jesus's light. Just as the moon (the "lesser light") reflects the light of the sun, so we reflect the light of the Son of God as we let our light shine. We manifest God's goodness working through us. Hasty deductions lead to false logic. Faulty logic leads to false conclusions. False conclusions lead to false teaching. And false teaching always divides the body of Christ.

To further clarify how violations of logic conquer and divide us, let us briefly return to the subject of alcohol. Most conservative Christians would likely embrace a strong conviction that drinking alcohol is wrong. The wiser, more spiritually mature Christians must not only be sober, but dry. They would agree that, while there is a time appointed for every event under heaven (Eccles. 3:1), there is never a time for partaking of alcohol. This statement sounds holy and does potentially have some biblical footing. If alcohol may cause a brother to stumble, "we then who are strong ought to bear with the scruples of the weak, and not to please ourselves" (Rom. 15:1). Abstinence from alcohol may seem logical. After all, look how prevalent is the devastation from over-indulgence in alcohol consumption. How many marriages have crumbled by it? How many lives have been lost to the drunken driver? Pity the child who is tormented by an abusive alcoholic parent. What good has ever come from alcohol? And so the arguments go. Such a renunciation may sound biblical but such a claim does not hold up logically. Total abstinence from alcohol is not a biblical teaching.

The primary admonition taught in the Bible is given in Paul's letter to the Ephesians. Here the apostle is emphasizing how Christians should walk carefully, as wise persons who should walk as children of light because of our conversion to Christ. He exhorts us to understand what the will of the Lord is: "and do not be drunk with wine, in which is dissipation" (Eph. 5:18). From this command we can logically deduce that getting drunk from wine was a real possibility. Since inebriation is the primary concern in that statement, obviously this wine that Paul was referring to was a true digestive ferment that yielded ethanol, or alcohol, as a byproduct of this fermentation. This is how wine is made. Alcohol gives wine its unique properties of taste and effect. Alcohol is the desired product in winemaking. Ethanol is able to cross a filter, called the blood-brain barrier, designed to protect the brain from harmful substances. When alcohol is consumed, it is absorbed into the bloodstream and contacts neurons in the brain, which change our behavior. Anyone who drinks a glass of wine is to some degree under the influence of alcohol. The more alcohol consumed, the greater its influence on the central nervous system. Simple observation teaches us that inebriation may cause undesired effects—indiscretion, verbosity, loosening of morals, crassness, violence, injuries, stupor, and even death. The first effect of alcohol consumption is compromised judgment. Hence the reason for free drinks in gambling casinos. Obviously then, all alcohol is harmful and morally wrong to consume. Right? Wrong.

To make such a claim is to disavow the Bible's own teaching. It also conflicts with current science. In recent years alcohol has been declared a carcinogen. The more you consume, the greater your risk of cancer. On the other hand, mild to moderate drinking has demonstrated a significant reduction in stroke, heart disease and diabetes[7]—all major causes of mortality in the United States. In other words, the non-drinker has a greater risk of dying from these three diseases than the person who consumes 1-2 drinks of alcohol per day. Stated another way, in small amounts, alcohol does have medicinal value. This research seems to support the well-known principle of moderation in all things. But is this statement supported in Scripture? To fairly answer that question, we must strictly adhere to principles of sound logic, and as always, put aside all scripturally unfounded biases.

We are clearly given the negative command to not be intoxicated with alcohol. Another abiding principle for Christians is given in Romans 14 where Paul instructs us in lessons on Christian liberty. He emphasizes the importance of being sensitive to the weak consciences of some Christian brothers. The Christian who is weak in faith may also have a weak conscience, and the more mature Christian is cautioned to not judge the weaker brother because of his opinions, which may include ingesting or not ingesting that which God has declared to be not forbidden, not wrong to consume. But while Paul declares such liberties legal and intrinsically of no offense, he also asserts, "It is good neither to eat meat nor drink wine nor do anything by which your brother stumbles or is offended" (Rom. 14:21). Is it wrong to eat meat? No. Is drinking a little wine wrong? No. Paul affirms that nothing is unclean in itself (Rom. 14:14), and this includes meat and wine. Keep in mind that the *weaker* brother is the one who considers something to be wrong because of appearances or possible association of a substance with an unholy fellowship. Our goal as mature Christians should be to not cause any weaker brother to stumble in their spiritual walk. We should pursue peace and simultaneously build one another up in all truth. We should not state a lie, however, such as declaring that total abstinence from alcohol is a biblical teaching. It is not.

Consider Jesus's first miracle of converting water to wine (John 2:1-10). Pay careful attention to the setting. Jesus, His mother, and his disciples were invited to a wedding. It was a time to dance, a time for celebration, and yes, a time for drinking wine. People had been consuming wine during the festivities, and they obviously were not just sipping wine, because the wine gave out. They consumed all of it.

Mary brought the matter to her Son's attention, fully expecting Him to solve the problem. And He did. Jesus gave them an additional six twenty-gallon or thirty-gallon water pots full of some incredibly good tasting wine. Jesus performed this miracle in the presence of his mother and disciples. If alcohol consumption is intrinsically evil, then Jesus sinned in making wine for consumption. He certainly also set a poor example for His disciples. And would he not have been contributing to the delinquency of the wedding guests? Do you see the breakdown in logic of a Christian who teaches his children that all alcohol consumption is inherently of the devil?

The astute child is very apt to notice the discrepancy between the parent's opinion and what the Bible teaches. This demonizing of alcohol declares that Jesus was doing an evil work. It also discredits the apostle Paul who advised Timothy to "use a little wine for your stomach's sake and your frequent infirmities" (1 Tim. 5:23). Was Paul corrupting Timothy, his fellow Christian who was being instructed on how to shepherd a church? Obviously, this was not the case. A little wine could benefit Timothy; it has a calming effect. Therefore, we need to always deduce logically from Scripture every interpretation in order to rightly exegete any passage, principle, story or teaching.

For the sake of answering those who might suggest that this wine created by Jesus or suggested by Paul was not actually fermented, consider the biblical terms and contexts used. Wine and strong drink are linked thirteen times in the Old Testament, once in the New Testament. We read of new wine, *oínos néos* (recent vintage), and old wine, *oínos* (later vintage), both of which most commonly suggest a fermented product. Wine is elsewhere described as "blood of the grapes" and "fruit of the vine." The termed *gleúkos* (sweet wine) mentioned in Acts 2:13 was the drink the apostles were accused of imbibing, suggesting they were drunk at the feast of Pentecost. Wine does have medicinal benefits when taken in small amounts, as Paul suggested to Timothy. Any fermented vineyard product yields a predictable degree of alcohol based on its sugar content. The ancient fermentation process would yield the same percentage of alcohol as modern fermentation since the process of microbial fermentation is, regarding microbial physiology, identical in both eras. Wine only loses its potency when exposed to air, resulting in the oxidation of ethanol to ethanoic acid (acetic acid), otherwise known as vinegar, or in biblical parlance, "sour wine." Vinegar was used in cooking but does nothing to settle a stomach or calm the nerves. The ancients were no strangers to more potent brews as well. The Gospel of Luke tells us that John the baptizer would drink no wine or strong drink (Luke 1:15). Logic must always prevail. Logic demands that drinking alcohol must not be made a test of fellowship, any more than… eating meat.[8]

14. Incomplete Bible knowledge

Any church that is obedient to the Great Commission of reaching out to make disciples (Matt. 28:19) is going to have among its members some immature Christians needing a lot of nurturing in the faith. We all begin our Christian journey in infancy, having very limited Bible knowledge. Unfortunately, we have too many followers who have proclaimed the name of Christ for many years, but still have little command of the Scriptures. We all need regular spiritual nourishment if we are to grow in spiritual maturity, in the same way that we need a regular food supply to sustain our physical bodies.

Babes in the faith cannot be expected to know more than one who has professed Christ for many years. Neither will they always act properly, that is, in a way pleasing to God. They must be taught. Paul therefore places a great emphasis on discipleship. He spells out the requirements of an elder, not the least of which is being able to teach through sound doctrine and shepherd the flock. Although imperfect themselves, elders must know how to lead the immature Christian along the path of righteousness, and this requires that they study, learn and practice doing the word of God.

However, none of us has a total grasp on the Bible. You may recall Apollos, whom Luke refers to as "an eloquent man" and "mighty in the Scriptures" (Acts 18:24). Luke tells us, "This man had been instructed in the way of the Lord; and being fervent in spirit, he spoke and taught accurately the things of the Lord, though he knew only the baptism of John. So he began to speak boldly in the synagogue. When Aquila and Priscilla heard him, they took him aside and explained to him the way of God more accurately" (Acts 18:25-26).

Here was a man who had studied the Scriptures, was a powerful and effective speaker, and took seriously his mission of demonstrating by the Scriptures his proclamation that Jesus was the Messiah. But he hadn't heard about the baptism of the Holy Spirit. Remember, the New Testament was still in the process of being written at that time. So Apollos was taken aside (not openly ridiculed or humiliated), and was more thoroughly instructed in God's design in Christian conversion. His knowledge of the Scriptures was incomplete. Notice also that Apollos was not given a perfect explanation but a "more accurate" explanation. Nowhere does the Bible say Priscilla or Aquila spoke under inspiration of the Holy Spirit. Nonetheless, their teaching was important and it corrected a deficit in Apollos's understanding of God's Way. This passage serves as a good model for us as we seek a deeper and more complete understanding of God's word, and as we deal with those having less knowledge than we. We must both be open to a deeper understanding and have patience and sensitivity as we teach others. These attitudes create a unifying spirit in the church.

15. Sectarian devotion

A final consideration leading to serious interpretive errors is a blind devotion to a cause or group that does not allow for the true power of the Holy Spirit to work in us because of a refusal to consider any teaching not aligned with the norms of our doctrinal group affections. This selective obstinance is candidly seen in the publishing houses of the multitude of denominations.

The errors of groupthink are quickly palpable among naïve newcomers to a denomination who are not yet privy to the herd mentality that prevails in modern churchianity. Denominationalism, as previously discussed, is an overpowering obstacle to both the oneness of Christ's church body and to clear and sound Bible comprehension and teaching. This fact requires some careful soul searching, as nothing is more upsetting to the human psyche than to be told, even if by God Himself, that our affiliations are wrong. People generally do not respond well to a challenge to their belief system, even in the face of solid biblical evidence. This truth is even more magnified when supported by a group mentality that falsely allays our hidden insecurities. Ultimately, we sacrifice some degree of inner joy and emotional stability for wont of the status quo, as opposed to standing up for clear biblical teaching.

We must always remember that Jesus Christ, and He alone, is Head of His church. Anyone daring to undermine Jesus's authority as Head of the Body is clearly antagonistic to the global church of Christ. The church is a theocracy. It is not a democracy, not a dictatorship, not a socialist movement or any other form of government.

We now live in a day much like the Roman Empire when all religions were deemed acceptable. We of the church are pressured by a society that insists we offend nobody, and the church is caving to such compromise. Yes, the idiosyncrasies of denominations change over time, and we are presently seeing a grave trend toward accepting societal norms over biblical truths. Any deviation from a unified, Bible-based Christian church puts us on weaker ground, on a sandy foundation so contrary to that which Jesus had in mind. As soon as we declare ourselves a Lutheran, a Presbyterian, a Pentecostal, a Baptist, a Mennonite, an Episcopalian, or any other sect, we have offended our Savior. We have set ourselves apart from the universal brotherhood of Christ, the church body for which Jesus prayed would be one. Read again the words of the apostle Paul: "Now I plead with you, brethren, by the name of our Lord Jesus Christ, that you all speak the same thing, and that there be no divisions among you, but that you be perfectly joined together in the same mind and in the same judgment" (1 Cor. 1:10). The only way this can be achieved is to return to the plain and solid teachings of the Bible.

Given that we are all imperfect humans, unity will always be a struggle. But reuniting the Christian church is imperative. We must be willing and able to acknowledge our shortcomings, and commit to removing these barriers to unity through a strong devotion to a right biblical understanding. With these goals in mind, let us now proceed with a brief discourse on how to make God's words say exactly what He intended them to say and mean. Let's see if we can become better students of His word by heightening our awareness of these barriers to sound Bible interpretation, and by actively striving to put aside all forms of "I think" theology, all biases and willful misrepresentations. Let's approach the Bible with a blank slate mentality and ask afresh, what is God really saying? We begin this journey by summarizing and highlighting some elementary principles of interpretation that, if ignored, will only fester confusion and discord among the members of God's family. Sound interpretation is crucial to church unity. Nothing less will do.

Endnotes

[1] David Alexander and Patricia Alexander (eds.), *Eerdmans Handbook to the Bible*, Eerdmans, Grand Rapids, 1992.

[2] Merrill F. Unger, *The New Unger's Bible Dictionary*, Moody Press, Chicago, 1988.

[3] Henry M. Morris, *The Biblical Basis for Modern Science*, Master Books, Green Forest, AR, 2002.

[4] F. F. Bruce, *The Hard Sayings of Jesus*, Intervarsity Press, Downers Grove, IL, 1983.

[5] Jack Cottrell, *Gender Roles & the Bible*, College Press, Joplin, 1994.

[6] Justin Peters, "Clouds Without Water," <justinpeters.org>, accessed on June 14, 2019.

[7] Christopher Snowdon, "The Great Alcohol Cover-Up," February 10, 2016, <health.spectator.co.uk>, accessed on April 07, 2019.

[8] On a personal note, as a physician I do not advocate consumption of alcohol to those who have chosen abstinence simply because no one knows if he or she might succumb to excesses of this substance. I have voiced to my own children many a stern warning regarding the potential abuse of alcohol (and other substances). This said, I also have strived to teach them exactly what that Bible says about the use of alcohol, and it has served my children well.

Chapter 9

Basic Principles of Sound Interpretation

We now begin a review of what is generally considered the essential principles of sound interpretation. For some of you this may be completely new information, for others a good review. Reading and studying a few good textbooks on Bible interpretation is a most worthwhile endeavor, and every student of the Bible is encouraged to ardently study hermeneutics. Also of great value is studying the original Bible languages, although for most people in a busy routine this is not practicable.

The following basic but essential principles of Bible interpretation are not exhaustive or complete by any means, and this chapter is not intended to be a substitute for the fine works of authors who delve into the technical and elaborate rules of Bible interpretation. Every evangelist, theologian, elder, preacher, teacher, new convert and genuine Christian disciple ought to spend time in the serious study of God's word in obedience to Jesus's imperative that we receive proper instruction in "all that I commanded you" (Matt. 28:20). This is how real disciples are made.

The following text is written with a dual intent: 1) to summarize the critical points of interpretive skills necessary to avoid the most common mistakes made when reading and trying to make sense out of Scripture, and 2) to demonstrate through clear examples how sound interpretation is essential to the unity of all Christians. For this reason, I have specifically chosen to address some divisive topics along the way in order to elucidate why we are so strongly divided, and to highlight the importance of adhering to the rules of sound interpretation so we might think alike. Our goal is to have the mind of Christ. Like-mindedness is a product of Christ centeredness. I challenge you to shelve your denominational creed and respect what the Bible really has to say about these points that divide us. If this chapter makes understanding the Bible a little easier and opens your eyes to the ways in which churches divide and delude one another on misconstrued doctrinal issues, then it shall have served its purpose.

As you are reading, keep in mind those fifteen common errors made when interpreting the Bible. If you feel in any way threatened or intimidated by what you are reading (and at some point you likely shall), ask yourself why such emotions are stirred. Then I ask you to think your position afresh, let down your defenses, and ask a simple question: what does the Bible really say? You may find it helpful to discuss your feelings with a fellow Christian. Do remember to be Berean in your pursuit of truth. A Berean-minded Christian is a unifying Christian. And finally, have some fun along the way. Studying the Bible is exciting, and it can produce much good fruit in our lives. The more we know God, the more we can rejoice in what He has done for us, and the greater is our potential to bring forth good works worthy of our calling. Let's begin!

Exegesis Versus Eisegesis

A chief axiom of all Bible interpretation is that we search out the exact meaning of a scriptural passage rather than assign our own meaning to the text. *Exegesis* is simply an accurate translation and exposition of the ancient writings. Good exegesis means deriving an exact meaning of what the author intended to communicate. In contrast, *eisegesis* occurs when a reader formulates his own meaning or interpretation of a passage and forces that meaning into the text, giving no regard to context or what the author really meant to communicate. It is the deadliest of all interpretive flaws, making the Bible say whatever *you* want it to say.

Eisegesis is a trap that ensnares far too many preachers and teachers. Even many with good intentions are led astray by the error of Scripture twisting, and it must be avoided at all cost. No mortal has the authority to impose his or her own meaning on a sacred teaching whose authenticity was designed and protected by the Holy Spirit. We are sufficiently warned in Scripture that those who distort the message of God do so at great peril to themselves. Willful eisegesis begets the wrath of God. Exegesis, on the other hand, always confers a blessing to the discerning reader and hearer. It promotes knowledge and wisdom from above rather than from whimsical man. Eisegesis is the tool of the false teacher, the deceiver, the enemy of God. No amount of false piety or claim to scholarship shall ever pardon the false prophet.

What are some examples of eisegesis? Here's one: God told Hosea to "take to yourself a wife of harlotry" (Hosea 1:2). Since God gave a prophet this command, then harlotry must be an act condoned by God. Why else would God advise a prophet to marry a prostitute? This is eisegesis. It completely ignores the context of Hosea's message.

Another illustration of eisegesis would be the claim that we must sell all our property and possessions because that's what the early church did. We seldom hear any preaching on this passage because it scares us half to death. The truth is, this is not what the early Christians did. The Christian brotherhood had no resemblance to Communism or communal living. It does, however, take seriously the important teaching of taking care of those in need.

Most of us have labored hard for our property and possessions, and the suggestion that we must give up all our possessions by design of the early church is too huge a pill to swallow. But if you read closely, Acts 2:45 doesn't say that they sold *all* their property and *all* their possessions. That would make no sense, since they would all be homeless and without any resources remaining for personal sustenance and future generosity. How many of us has ever donated a car or given an item for a church fundraiser? Have you ever heard of Christians donating a piece of property that became a church camp? Donating or selling something for the good of the church doesn't mean we must all get rid of everything we own and become impecunious vagabonds. It means we are willingly giving up something for the good of the church or to further the Gospel message. To the extent that we are materially blessed, and out of the sheer goodness of our hearts, we give. God doesn't need our gifts to grow his church, but He did make financial giving a regular part of Christian fellowship for our own good.

The apostle Paul told the Ephesian elders, "You yourselves know that these hands have provided for my necessities, and for those who were with me. I have shown you in every way, by laboring like this, that you must support the weak. And remember the words of the Lord Jesus, that He said, 'It is more blessed to give than to receive'" (Acts 20:34-35). Paul worked hard as a means of providing for himself (so as to be no burden on others) and for those accompanying him, and we are reminded here to not be lazy or burden others when we are fully capable of working. We also are reminded to help those incapable of taking care of themselves, for in giving we receive the greater blessing. The message of Acts 2:45 is that Christians should take care of one another in time of need. It is not an imperative to forsake all possessions and take up a vow of poverty.

Unfortunately, the blunders of eisegesis have produced a mountain of popular Christian beliefs totally unfounded in Scripture.

Some of them even pertain to the way of salvation. Ask most Christians how they were saved, and they will tell you, "I asked Jesus into my heart." Such a response is wholly a product of eisegesis. Where in the Bible is a Christian convert ever told to ask Jesus into his heart as a means of salvation? The idea likely comes from an improper interpretation of Revelation 3:20. "Behold, I stand at the door and knock. If anyone hears my voice and opens the door, I will come in to him and dine with him, and he with Me." The reader must recall that John was addressing Christians in "the seven churches" (Rev. 1:4), not the unsaved, and no reference is made to unconverted sinners asking Jesus into the heart. If we can't get the facts straight on so essential a doctrine as salvation, then we are clearly in trouble. Eisegesis always leads to disorder. A good eisegete is an author of confusion who wrongfully divides the churches of the saints. Countless millions of Christians are unwitting victims of eisegesis.

In order to better understand why the error of eisegesis is so popular, we need to understand human nature. Why would any sincere follower of Christ want to inject their own meaning into the sacred writings? One reason may be that we want solid answers to all our spiritual questions. The Bible is nebulous at times, requiring us to dig deeply into the Scriptures to obtain a clear understanding of spiritual things. We all generally have a fear of the unknown. Not having all the answers makes us uncomfortable. The untenable questions to the things that we fear confer on Bible readers an irresistible urge to "fill in the blanks," or to speculate on a scriptural reference that is not solidly or clearly defined. For example, John the apostle never uses the word "antichrist" in his writing of the book of Revelation. Yet he defines for us "the spirit of the antichrist" in his first letter (1 John 4:3), and he affirmed at the time of writing this letter (toward the end of the first century) that many antichrists had already come (1 John 2:18).

Despite this straightforward teaching, the popular thought is that the beast of Revelation is a reference to *the one and only Antichrist.* If we are told that there are many antichrists, and that many anti-christs have already come, then the notion of having only one anti-christ who will rise up at the final battle of Armageddon cannot be accurate. Neither is it correct to say that future antichrists shall not come. The "man of sin" referenced in 2 Thessalonians 2:3-4 certainly fits the definition of an antichrist, one who is described as "the son of perdition, who opposes and exalts himself above all that is called God or that is worshiped, so that he sits as God in the temple of God, showing himself that he is God." Whoever this man is, he sounds like he might be the chief of all antichrists—past, present and future.

One can hardly resist speculating on who this son of perdi-tion shall be. The suspense of not knowing plagues us. Long ago, Nero was awarded the nefarious title. In more modern times, some thought Hitler was the Antichrist. Others have believed the papacy shall produce this final evil despot. But all such proposals are spec-ulation, and dogmatic speculation is indeed a form of eisegesis, however doctrinaire the assertions.

Admittedly, these prognostications can be entertaining and even somehow comforting. They might serve to heighten our sense of discernment, so as to not be naively led astray. This passage in 2 Thessalonians likely has led to more speculation among Bible scholars than any other. But as soon as we transition from "I sup-pose" to "I believe," we excavate another fork of division on unity road. Dogma divides. Unnecessary dogma divides unnecessarily. It is far better that we maintain a unifying spirit based on clear biblical revelation than split over unfounded beliefs and unverifi-able hypotheses. The identity of this wretched imposter shall one day be revealed, so we are told in Second Thessalonians 2:3, but no one can accurately nominate this person before he is revealed. We are specifically told to avoid such presage because our prideful opinions always cause confusion and schisms. For this reason, Paul warned the disorderly Corinthian Christians, "Learn in us not to think beyond what is written, that none of you may be puffed up on behalf of one against the other" (1 Cor. 4:6).

Exegesis demands that we speak lucidly what the Bible clearly teaches, and that we avoid dogmatizing speculative assumptions that are not distinctly propounded by God. Rather than submit ourselves to the accursed folly of eisegetical whim, perhaps we should choose silence over prognostication. In doing so, we avoid unnecessary disputes over things in doubt, deflecting possible division over a false test of fellowship. When reading the Bible we must always extract meaning and never infuse our own ideas or opinions as Bible doctrine. To have ideas or opinions about what may ensue is very natural, but to make any opinion a test of fellowship is divisive. When listening to a speaker, we must always discern if we are hearing the message the Holy Spirit intended us to hear, lest we have our own ears tickled at the cost of counterfeit faith.

Context Is King!

The entirety of the Bible, Old Testament and New Testament, is context. No book of the Bible can be evaluated completely apart from considering the context of every other book in the Bible. No principle supersedes or negates another principle unless the Bible clearly affirms it. No doctrine of faith can be isolated apart from the entirety of the Bible. Every word, every phrase, every sentence, every book of both Old and New Testaments, comprise the full context. The preacher or Bible study teacher must understand the necessity of taking any point of what is written within the scope and framework of a passage in light of every other passage of Scripture. If we lose sight of the immediate purpose of the passage, the explicit intent for which it was drafted, then we are likely to distort the message.

Likewise, if we isolate any passage apart from all others, we may misrepresent the author and, in a very real sense, we become false teachers. The most immediate burden of good interpretation is to consider carefully what immediately precedes and what follows a given passage. From there, the interpreter should expand to other similar passages, called *parallels*, that deal with the same subject and use similar language in order to better solidify the meaning. A. Berkeley Mickelsen presents a concise five-point summary of principles for interpreting from context.[1] He keenly asserts that the smaller the passage, the greater the risk of distorting the context.

In order to get the most information out of any passage of Scripture, one must consider the historical setting, the genre of writing, customs practiced at the time of writing, and the purpose for which the words were written. We can only make sense of historical writings to the extent that we know and understand the world in which the authors lived. Ramm defines this problem as the *culture-gap* between our times and biblical times which the translator and interpreter must bridge.[2] He rightly concludes, "Until we can recreate and understand the cultural patterns of the various Biblical periods we will be handicapped in our understanding of the fuller meaning of Scripture."[3]

For example, when reading about battles and military conquests in the Bible, we will find no military doctrine of air superiority using high-technology fighter aircraft, or any description of tank battalions or submarine warfare. They didn't exist. We rather read of chariots, spears, swords, stones and shields. When the apostle Paul speaks of the government's law enforcement method of meting out justice in Romans 13:4, he warns not of a judgment by lethal injection or the electric chair, but rather declares that the Roman government having judicial authority "does not bear the sword in vain" (Rom. 13:4). The sword was an instrument of lethal punishment in the Roman Empire, and this verse must be understood in that context in order to gain the import of the writer's words. The

Bible must be read and understood through the eyes of the writer living in his world. Otherwise, we may not understand the meaning of a passage. Historical-cultural ignorance almost always results in a distortion of its intended meaning.

A fine example of misrepresentation of Scripture can be demonstrated by both internal and external evidence (that is, proofs within and outside of the Bible) as we look at Paul's letter to the church at Corinth. What is the context of First Corinthians? First, the letter is written in the New Testament, and the setting is in the early Church Age, meaning Jesus has ascended to heaven and the Holy Spirit has been given as a seal of eternal life to those who profess Jesus as their Savior. Second, the letter is addressed to members of the local church in Corinth. He is talking to fellow Christians. From external historical writings, we know that the city of Corinth was far less than moral and upright in its daily affairs. It was a sailor's town, a debauched city that reveled in its lasciviousness and corruption. The church in this city consisted of professing Christians, not of unbelieving Jews or Greeks. These Christians were being influenced by a number of sordid cults and a glut of unwholesome influences.

Third, Paul is writing the letter to deal with specific and serious problems that were rearing their ugly heads within this church's doors. Thus, anything read from this letter must be understood in the context of Paul correcting and chastising an unruly church body. If its purpose and setting are not clearly understood and kept in mind as we read the letter, all sorts of misunderstandings (and eisegesis) will surface. These points of context must be retained in the forefront of our brains at all times if we are to avoid perverting or twisting any verse of Scripture from this letter. Paul begins the letter by thanking God for His grace bestowed on the Corinthians and then gets right to the point, stating his main purpose for the letter. He expresses his appalling disdain for the quarrels and divisions among them. He then proceeds with an emphatic denouncement of the specific causes of all this division.

Here we are actually given a very early account of denominationalism and its associated evils. Paul's response to this division is clearly not one of affirmation, but of reprobation. When we adhere to the proper context, we can learn much from all the specific problems of this local Corinthian church, as we see many of the same problems arising in our churches today. Therefore, Paul's admonitions apply every bit as much to us now as they did to this first-century church. But not everything in that time correlates to the twenty-first-century church.

The New Testament obviously was still being penned by Paul and others, so they did not have the benefit of a completed revelation from God. That is significant because unlike them, we *do* have a completed work of God's written communication to mankind, called the Holy Bible. On the other hand, we no longer have among us any of the original apostles, or those on whom they laid hands for a specific purpose. This fact has much significance in deriving an accurate and proper interpretation of the Book of First Corinthians. However, many of the Corinthian church problems still afflict us today.

The first problem of divisions among them that Paul addressed has ballooned in our day, and stricken us like the bubonic plague. If we adhere to the integrity of the Bible context, we must conclude that any and all modern-day divisions of Christ's body are no less frowned upon by God than were the divisions of the church at Corinth. This conclusion demands that we borrow from another rule of interpretation that shall be discussed later in this chapter, but the overriding principle is that division is wrong. Christ is not divided, and neither should be we who profess Him as the Head of our church. In the same way, we must forever and diligently keep in mind the immediate and the broad context of any referenced Bible passage.

Scripture should also be interpreted with Scripture, because all of Scripture is the sum of context. When the meaning of an isolated passage of Scripture is in question, we should look to the Scriptures to explain it. A great mistake of many teachers and preachers is to start by heading to Bible commentaries in order to grasp a better understanding of a book or passage.

Commentaries are the written conclusions of others who have presumably done their diligent study. However diligent the scholarship, every commentary is branded by the author's own biases, subtle or camouflaged though they may be. As such, commentaries should probably be our last source in seeking Bible knowledge. They also should always be carefully screened to see if the author's conclusions are solidly based in Scripture. Not all commentaries are bad, but they are a compilation of thoughts and ideas from an uninspired writer who may introduce his own biases and misunderstandings of a Bible book. We avoid this potential misdirection by first searching out all passages of Scripture that pertain to a given principle, thought, teaching or verse. When the proper rules of context are followed, errors and divisions melt away.

Adherence to the Rules of Human Language

As previously stated, written communication is a purely human trait bestowed upon us by our Creator. Writing affords an enduring record of the spoken word. When Jesus walked the earth, He spoke many things. Were it not for the recording of these words by scribes, we would have no idea what He said. William Strunk, renowned grammarian and author of *The Elements of Style*, makes an interesting point about writing. He states, "Vigorous writing is concise. A sentence should contain no unnecessary words, a paragraph no unnecessary sentences."[4]

Any student who ever has been assigned a 500-word composition knows that writing is hard work. We can easily understand

and appreciate the role of the Holy Spirit in delivering to us a perfectly edited compilation of sacred writings, whereby the finished work contained not a single unnecessary word. It also contained no inaccurate words, no fallacious words, and no undesirable words or sentences. God chose to reveal to us through a written document all that we know about Him and His will for us. He saw fit in His wisdom to use words written in three languages (Hebrew, Aramaic, Greek) to communicate all that He wanted us to know.

These words of the Bible are assembled logically according to the basic rules of grammar, rules that are fundamental to every human language so we can make sense of the text. We have rules for nouns, pronouns, verbs, adverbs, adjectives, articles, conjunctions, prepositions and clauses. We are guided by rules of syntax (sentence structure) and rules for punctuation; rules for tense; rules for superlatives and comparatives. Every human language requires strict adherence to these rules in order for the words or characters to make sense. Without these rules, we have returned to Babel. If not for these rules of human language, how could we communicate in written form? Without such rules, we convey nothing but nonsense. The corollary to this premise is that if we manipulate these rules, then meaning is lost, and anything goes. Much like the research scientist who skews his observations and produces false data, the reader who neglects the rules of human language misrepresents the author's intended meaning.

When applied to Scripture, the consequences of strictly following these rules are no small matter, as they may affect our eternal fate. We also have no hope for Christian unity if we cannot think and say the same things. In 1999, NASA lost a 125 million dollar probe to Mars because of not speaking the same thing. When exchanging vital data before launch, engineers failed to convert from English to metric measurements. Miscommunication is costly.

If we fail to speak the same thing, then we are divided. The most serious dilemma of the ecumenical movement or any unity quest is finding common ground. At the very foundation of this ground must be a prerequisite and logical basis for approaching God in His revelation to us. We have bestowed to us in this Church Age the completed Scriptures that must be read and interpreted in such a way that the message is not lost or distorted. One who brings good news to those who have never heard the message of salvation needs only to read pertinent words of Scripture to forever change a person's life. Many times, no explanation is even necessary. Assuming the hearer is literate, the message will be understood by the listener who has at least a rudimentary grasp of his native tongue.

When questions arise, as they always do, we may opt to simply quote other Scriptures for clarification, or we might offer an explanation or clarification of the message. No problem is inherently caused by the one who simply reads a Bible passage, but the hearer himself may fail to abide by the rules of human language as he listens to the message. False conclusions may prevail. The message of salvation is so simple and straightforward that it can (and should) stand on its own. But legitimate questions do arise about the path to salvation, and human interaction occurs primarily by dialogue. This is where the sincere evangelist must take seriously his or her commitment to following rules of human language.

Even when directly reading a gospel passage to someone, the hearer's own biases, intellectual limitations, lack of cultural understanding, and his own sinful nature, may introduce distortions of the text. These can so easily nullify the impact of the message, failing to allow the life-giving words given by the Spirit of God to have their effect. Insincerity abounds. The earnest seeker of eternal life will legitimately ask for clarification, amplification, and application regarding the Christian life. This interaction is an integral means of making disciples. Effective discipleship begins by keeping the message of salvation simple and straightforward, and abiding by solid rules of grammar when teaching the Bible. The idea that the Bible is such a lofty work that grammatical accuracy need not apply is fallacy. This heretical notion is the work of the false teacher and apostate.

Many Bible expositors and preachers nonetheless feel compelled to mystify the Bible. In doing so they readily put aside these basic rules of human language, perhaps feeling that such rules aren't good enough for the word of God. In fact, the opposite is true. Others may slovenly and mistakenly claim to rely on the Holy Spirit to guide them to the right interpretation. This is false piety. However well-intentioned their sentiments, these teachers corrupt God's message in the process of ignoring rules of language.

While we must vehemently affirm the uniqueness of the Bible over all other writings, it is still recorded according to the normal rules of written communication, just like any other book. Such a statement does nothing to detract from the supreme position the Bible holds among all other literary works. The Bible is fully inspired by God. It is literally "God-breathed" (Gr. *theopneustós*); and the power of God's inspiration is revealed by its harmony and conclusive salvific nature. We must also remember that the power of the Holy Spirit is manifest in words set forth in human language so that anyone having a grasp of the language can understand the words.

To ignore the rules of grammar when reading the Bible is to dishonor the Spirit by warping the message. The work of the Holy Spirit does not stop with inspiration, but God obviously saw fit to bestow us with all the knowledge of His nature and will through words. Without the written record of Scripture we would know nothing of God's special revelation to us, including His will and His plan of salvation. This method of communication was God's choice, not ours. The word *scriptural* refers to a written transfer of information. Anything written to confer knowledge and meaning must follow rules of human language. Anything less produces mumbo jumbo, a word salad, a calligraphical cesspool. Such is not the deific work of the Holy Spirit.

Words Have Meaning

The understanding of words in Scripture is so important to our understanding of the Bible that one could easily write an entire book on this subject alone. In fact, some excellent scholars have already undertaken this great task. Here I wish not to define specific words, but to show just how important a single word can be in formulating ideas about God, the Bible, and about the divisiveness that can result from a poor understanding of a single word.

The New Testament was written in the *koiné*, the commonly spoken Greek vernacular of the Mediterranean world during Jesus's time on earth. Koiné was spoken for a period of about 600 years, roughly from 300 BC to AD 300. The beauty of this fact is that *koiné* is a dead language. It is no longer used, and thus the meaning of words in the k*oiné* can never be changed. Therefore, if we look up the word "repentance" in the Bible, we can readily define the meaning and see how the word specifically was used with regard to salvation. Some Greek words have more than one meaning, and in such cases we draw on the rules of word usage in light of its context. The *koiné* may also use multiple words to more clearly define an idea, whereas in the English language we only have one word. For example, in the Greek language the English word "love" is further classified into four different types or categories of love. In English we must use a modifier word to distinguish between unconditional love, brotherly love, parental love and erotic love. The Greek language has a separate word for each. If we are unaware of this fact, we may lose the full or clearer meaning of a passage.

Stating the obvious is essential when the obvious is frequently ignored. For this reason, I must emphatically state that *words have meaning*. I wish to emphasize this point because so often confusion and discord arise from using a word too loosely, paying no attention to the original meaning of the word (etymology), or by not respecting the explicit purpose or setting associated with the word. This is precisely why we see so much confusion about, say, Christian baptism and baptism of the Holy Spirit.

Assigning one's own meaning to a word (yes, that would be eisegesis) is a common but cardinal flaw of sound interpretation. Our goal should be to define a word according to the author's definition, as he understood and meant the word to be used. As might be expected, denominations frequently abuse the word baptism in order to raise the banner of their quasi-cultic assertions. This is dangerous. If any confusion arises about the meaning of a word, then the serious Bible student must investigate its definition(s) with all diligence, using good reference books and all reliable resources at hand, in order to come to an accurate understanding of what the word means and how it is used in its proper context. Equally disdaining is the selective ignoring or downplaying of a word because it makes us uncomfortable or does not jive with our established denominational assertions.

Take the word *miracle*. Here we have a word that has been so profoundly abused that the word miracle has become almost meaningless in modern parlance. We have heard of miracle supplements and miracle cures, miracle foods and miracle hair and skin products. Listen to talk radio on Saturday mornings, and you'll hear all kinds of new miracle products being pedaled by modern-day magicians, wizards and charlatans. Here's a simple word of advice: Don't purchase any product advertised as being miraculous. All such claims are a sure-fire guarantee you are being scammed.

Vine's Expository Dictionary (online), defines the Greek word miracle (*dúnamis*) as follows: "'power, inherent ability,' is used of works of a supernatural origin and character, such as could not be produced by natural agents and means."[5] In other words, a miracle is a blatant and unequivocal manifestation of divine intervention leading to a disruption of the natural laws of physics. A miracle is a willful, God-caused supernatural phenomenon. The word commonly occurs biblically in the company of signs and wonders of God's authority and power. When "the sun stood still in the midst of heaven, and did not hasten to go down for about a whole day" (Joshua 10:13), that was a miracle. The earth does not naturally stop its rotation and orbiting around the sun. When Moses stretched out his hand and parted the Red Sea and the Israelites walked on dry land across the sea, that also was a miracle (Exod. 14:21-22). When Jesus or an apostle raised the dead, those were true miracles that defied all natural laws. The effect of miracles was immediate, publicly displayed, and clearly evident to all observers. God got directly involved and willfully altered the natural course of what otherwise would have happened under the prevailing laws of the physical universe.

In modern lingo, people have attributed many *natural* events to being "a miracle." This is actually a form of hyperbole, or exaggeration for the sake of emphasis, usually because of an emotional uprising within the soul caused by the magnificence of the event. With tears of joy family members witness the birth of a baby and call it a miracle. A soldier returns home after a protracted war and proclaims, "It's a miracle that I'm still here." The observant gardener watches her flowers blossom and declares the unfolding of a flower's petals to be nothing less than a miracle. Almost everyone has heard of someone, or possibly experienced firsthand, a "close-call" event that had every potential to be catastrophic, but it wasn't. With the utmost piety the near-victim asserts, "It was a miracle that I wasn't killed."

All such claims are deeply heartfelt, but completely erroneous. The birth of a baby is a very natural event. After the Creation, God told us to be fruitful and multiply, and all living things have naturally done so since the command was given. Anyone who has observed the birth of a child, or even a barnyard animal, has witnessed a delightful event, but not a miraculous one. The natural beauty observed throughout God's world is profound, but flowering is a very habitual occurrence of plant life.

The soldier who returned unharmed from war did so because the trajectory of bullets flying through the air did not intercept the space filled by the soldier's body—unless his safe return from war was an affirmative answer to someone's prayer. Many other soldiers of prayer did not have such a favorable outcome. The Bible has much to say about the power of prayer, and I fully affirm the Bible's claim that God *does* answer prayer. But answered prayer can never be positively authenticated. We have no way of proving it. However heartfelt our conviction that God has affirmatively answered our supplication, such answers cannot be scientifically proven. Let me restate this fact for emphasis and clarity. We may firmly believe our prayers are answered and strongly believe in the power of prayer, but we can never absolutely prove any outcome to be an answered prayer. A lack of proof does not necessarily negate a fact, but believing that God answered your prayer affirmatively must always, in the absence of evidence, be an act of faith. We must also realize that most men in the heat of battle are praying for deliverance and safety, but many are still killed despite their prayers. And that could just as well be an answered prayer. Sometimes God says no. War is dangerous. And we cannot manipulate God simply because we insist on a desirable outcome. God offers us no such promise or guarantee in this life.

Now let's analyze the near fatality. We grossly err when we assign a miraculous event to a near-miss collision. As I was discussing the purpose of miracles with a brother in Christ recently, he related a familiar near-miss story that I have heard many times in various forms. He was offended by my suggestion that this was not a miracle, but the statement was not made to put him on the defensive. I asked that he permit me to share my own story in the hopes of deflecting his angst.

A week after graduating from high school, I departed on a motorcycle trip from Rhode Island to Canada. On the back roads in the Canadian wilderness I was taking in all the beautiful scenery, cruising along and not paying much attention to the road since only one car was well ahead of me on this spacious country road. In my carelessness, I hadn't noticed that the car had come to a full stop, signaling a left turn. When my eyes drifted back to the road this car was some 20-30 feet ahead of me. I instinctively braked and fishtailed to the right. I saw my motorcycle foot pedal whiz by the car's right rear bumper, just inches away. It was one of those "My whole life flashed before me!" events. Pondering the near mishap later, I thanked God that I did not ram into the back of that car at 65 miles per hour. It would certainly have been sudden death. Was this near miss a miracle? Not at all. I call it a last-minute salvage reaction by a careless motorcyclist. Now if God had levitated my motorcycle above the car and gently dropped me down on the other side of the car—*that* would have been a miracle. If I had prayed for safety on the trip, and because of that prayer, the driver of the car wasn't there because she decided to stop and get gas before my arrival in her vicinity—*that* would have been an answered prayer, a result of God's benevolent providence. But I would have had no idea that God affirmatively answered my prayer. My salvaging of a bad scenario that resulted from my own negligence was not a miracle. It was a fortunate outcome resulting from my own initiative to instinctively use the laws of physics to my own advantage. Nothing more.

Now I fully realize some of you at this point may be bristling because you have wholeheartedly cherished such a "miracle" in your own life for years. You have considered your "rescue" as your own precious gift from God, and perceive a need to defend God's honor because you just *know* He interceded on your behalf. You might be thinking, "Who are you to tell me that when that car missed hitting me by one small inch, it wasn't a miracle?" Well, that leads to my next point. Do you remember that trite statement I made earlier? Words have meaning.

We must now reconcile the fact that words also have purpose. Let me illustrate with another word. The word baptize (*baptízō*) in the Greek, according to A. Oepke, means "to dip in or under," "to dye," "to immerse," "to sink," "to drown," "to bathe," "to wash."[6] That's its plain definition in common historical usage. But when applied to Christian baptism, the word signifies dipping, or immersion. Christian baptism not only has a meaning, it also has a purpose. When Jesus commanded us to go and make disciples, He said to baptize them in the name of the Father and the Son and the Holy Spirit, and then to teach them (Matt 28:19-20). Baptize, teach. We also see this command carried out in the nascent church. "Then those who had received his word were baptized; and that day about three thousand souls were added to them" (Acts 2:41). What was the purpose of this baptism? Understanding the purpose of a word is equally as important as understanding its meaning. In order to understand the full meaning and purpose of Christian baptism, we must examine all other passages that deal with this subject. In Romans 6:3 we read of such a purpose when Paul asks, "Do you not know that as many of us as were baptized into Christ Jesus were baptized into His death?" Paul further explains the purpose in the following verse. "Therefore we were buried with Him through baptism into death, that just as Christ was raised from the dead by the glory of the Father, even so we also should walk in newness of life" (Rom. 6:4).

The apostle Peter adds more light to the purpose of Christian baptism when he uses the saving of Noah's family who "were brought safely through the water" as an analogy. He purposes baptism to be "an antitype which now saves us," and "an appeal to God for a good conscience." Since this is not a discourse on the purpose of Christian baptism, I shall leave it to the reader to further investigate this purpose. But given the command by Jesus to baptize

Christian converts, we would be foolish to consider the purpose of baptism unimportant or superfluous in the setting of conversion. Baptism was clearly an integral part of the conversion process, and to deny or reject this command, one must resort to eisegesis.

The same must be said of the *purpose* of miracles. Most genuine Christians believe that the purpose of miracles is primarily to demonstrate the goodness of God. Jesus healed the sick, gave sight to the blind, cured the lame, raised the dead and likely performed thousands of miracles that were never recorded. John concludes his Gospel by recalling, "There are also many other things that Jesus did, which if they were written one by one, I suppose that even the world itself would not contain the books that would be written" (John 21:25).

Since Jesus performed so many miracles, Christians just assume that miracles are an ongoing part of Christianity today. But Jesus did not perform miracles *primarily* as an act of philanthropy, mercy or kindness. In order to understand the true purpose of miracles, all we need do is look at what the Bible says in context where miracles were performed.

When God commissioned Moses to tell the Egyptian Pharaoh to let the children of Israel go out of the land, Moses was anything but eager to accommodate. He reminded God of his own personal inadequacies and queried, "But suppose they will not believe me or listen to my voice; suppose they say, 'The Lord has not appeared to you'" (Exod. 4:1). God then instructed Moses, "When Pharaoh speaks to you, saying 'Show a miracle for yourselves,' then you shall say to Aaron, 'Take you rod and cast it before Pharaoh, and let it become a serpent'" (Exod. 7:9).

This reveals the purpose of miracles. Miracles are signs of God's authority. Their explicit purpose is to authenticate the messenger and his message. Miracles are intended to convince the hearers that the message is from God and is true. A miracle's purpose is persuading someone to believe the message by offering proof positive that it is authentic and indisputably from God. Moses knew Pharaoh would doubt his word. Each of the ten miraculous plagues against Egypt was to convince the Egyptians that Moses did indeed come with a message from God. God performed the miracles with a stated purpose, "that you may know that there is none like Me in all the earth" (Exod. 9:14). By the end of the tenth plague, they knew. So did the Israelites who had previously doubted. "Thus Israel saw the great work which the Lord had done in Egypt; so the people feared the Lord, *and believed* the Lord and His servant Moses" (Exod. 14:31, italics mine). Every miracle ever performed had a similar purpose, to proclaim God's truth and to convince doubting and unbelieving people of God's power and authority over all people and all things.

Miracles were not intended primarily to physically benefit a blessed recipient, even a faithful one. This fact is evident by those who were not miraculously healed or saved. John the Baptizer, declared greatest of all prophets (Luke 7:28) and a cousin of Jesus, was beheaded. The twelve original apostles less one endured a martyr's death. The apostle Paul, who had raised the dead and healed the sick, left one of his own cohorts Trophimus sick in Miletus (2 Tim. 4:20). If Paul could raise the dead, why could he not heal a trusted and loyal friend who assisted him on a missionary journey in Asia Minor? Surely if miraculous healing was solely intended to bestow a blessing of healing for its own sake, Trophimus would have been a most worthy candidate of healing by Paul. But this did not happen. Paul left this ailing Greek companion behind because of his physical infirmity, not because Trophimus lacked faith or because he was somehow disqualified to receive such a blessing.

Once again, the purpose of miracles was to offer a way for a doubter or unbeliever to verify that a word or message did come from God. The miraculous healing of Trophimus simply did not meet this criterion. We see the same situation with Epaphroditis whom Paul fondly refers to as "my brother, fellow worker, and fellow soldier" (Phil. 2:25). Paul relates how Epaphroditis was "sick almost unto death, but God had mercy on him, and not on him only but on me also, lest I should have sorrow upon sorrow" (Phil. 2:27). Did Epaphroditis pray for healing? Likely he did, as well as did many others, including Paul. Paul could not miraculously heal Epaphroditis, or surely he would have gladly relieved the suffering of his fellow soldier. If Epaphroditis were to be healed, his healing would come not through a miracle, but by answered prayer. Likewise Timothy, whom Paul affectionately called "a true son in the faith" (1 Tim. 1:2), was not to receive any miraculous healing from the one who was granted power to heal the sick and raise the dead. Instead Paul advised Timothy, "No longer drink water only, but use a little wine for your stomach's sake and your frequent infirmities" (1 Tim. 5:23). Timothy needed no affirmation from God, therefore no miracle would be performed to heal him.

When we observe the fact of selective miraculous healings that were denied to some pillars of the faith, this demands that we honestly inquire of the purpose of miracles. If miracles served the purpose of healing all who suffered or all the faithful, then it raises the question of why those who were bestowed miraculous powers could not heal themselves or their own beloved companions afflicted with calamity and illness. Was it because of a "conflict of interest"? The meaning and purpose of miracles must be kept in focus.

Paul's three friends certainly had no need of personal authentication of Paul's apostleship or his message. They already knew Christ was Messiah. They harbored no doubts about Paul's election as an apostle of Jesus Christ. A miracle would have served no purpose to the Philippian Christians who already acknowledged the authority of Paul's inspired message. If Paul would have healed these three ill brothers in Christ, might he have been accused of showing partiality to the select few in the brotherhood? Would he have been charged with usurping his God-given power for his own selfish purpose? Possibly. But the most evident reason why Paul could not heal Trophimus, Epaphroditis, Timothy, or even himself, is because the purpose of miracles would have been betrayed. Indeed, Paul himself entreated the Lord three times (See 2 Cor. 12) to have his own unspecified "thorn in the flesh" (v.7) removed, but God said no. No miracle. No healing. The answer to Paul's prayer was simply no. Sometimes when the answer to prayer is no, we are somehow blessed. Paul regarded his physical affliction as "a messenger of Satan to buffet me, lest I be exalted above measure" (v. 7).

Jesus supported His negation of Paul's prayer by explaining to him, "My grace is sufficient for you, for My strength is made perfect in weakness" (v. 9). This response had its precious effect in molding Paul's heart. He didn't whine and moan. He didn't accuse his Master of cruelty. He didn't try to manipulate the situation. He asked for healing and God said no. He then yielded to his suffering, declaring, "Therefore I take pleasure in infirmities, in reproaches, in needs, in persecutions, in distresses, for Christ's sake; for when I am weak, then I am strong" (v. 10).

His response almost begs the question, why do we insist on prayers for healing, and not for suffering? As Paul wrestled with his weaknesses and insults and distresses, he came to a very sobering conclusion that warrants close attention, and perhaps meditation, by all sincere Christians. "And indeed, all who desire to live godly in Christ Jesus will be persecuted" (2 Tim. 3:12). Not only does suffering have a purpose, but some form of suffering is obviously an integral part of godly living. If everything always went our way, we would have no perceived need. Saul the persecutor became Paul the apostle after Jesus got his attention by blinding him and showing him how many things he would suffer for the sake of Christ (Acts 9:8, 16). Let's get more personal. What is your affliction? Does it really hinder you from serving the purpose of God or could your suffering serve as a channel through which God has recruited you for His service?

Perhaps we should consider one other prayer God answered in the negative. In Gethsemane, Jesus Himself "knelt down and began to pray, saying, 'Father, if it is Your will, take this cup away from Me; nevertheless not My will, but Yours, be done'" (Luke 22:42). Even Jesus, in His full humanity, wished to avoid suffering. He certainly was no masochist, but His first priority was still the will of His Father. Notice what happened next. "Now an angel from heaven appeared to Him, strengthening Him" (Luke 22:43). How comforting and insightful is this statement, no doubt given for our benefit. Suffering is a given fact under the burden of our sinful world, but as we suffer for the purpose of God, we are always comforted. Suffering for God always serves a higher objective. Can you imagine where we'd be today if the Father would have removed Jesus's suffering and death on the cross?

Some of you may argue that faith in God did sometimes lead to a miraculous healing, and therefore our faith may do the same. This is a dangerous and untenable position to hold. The occasional report of healing a faithful petitioner is true, as we see in the account of Bartimaeus receiving his sight. We read in Luke 18:35-43 the story of Jesus approaching Jericho with "a multitude" when blind Bartimaeus cries out, "Jesus, Son of David, have mercy on me!" He begged to regain his sight.

Jesus responded by miraculously restoring his sight and stating, "Your faith has made you well." But notice the result. Bartimaeus "followed Him, glorifying God. And all the people, when they saw it, gave praise to God." This healing verified that Jesus was whom He declared Himself to be — the Son of God. The purpose of the miracle was still requisite, and its purpose was served. We must be very cautious about misinterpreting such historical miraculous events and mistakenly claiming for ourselves the same blessing by taking words out of context. This is wrongful and shoddy interpretation.

As we scrutinize miraculous events recorded throughout the Bible, we observe a repeated pattern. A message is first proclaimed, then the message is authenticated by a miracle. This results in some hearers believing the message. When Jesus performed His first miracle of converting water to wine, the result was very clear. "This beginning of signs Jesus did in Cana of Galilee, and manifested His glory; and His disciples believed in Him" (John 2:11).

These disciples once asked Jesus, "What shall we do, that we may work the works of God?" and Jesus replied, "This is the work of God, that you believe in Him whom He has sent." Their next question again highlights the purpose of miracles. "What then do You do for a sign, that we may see, and believe You?" (See John 6:25-30).

The repeated pattern is: miracle—see—believe. The primary goal of every miracle performed was belief. Once a person received authentication of the message, further miraculous confirmation was no longer necessary. This fact is stated in the story of the rich man and Lazarus. When the rich man petitioned Father Abraham to send Lazarus to warn the rich man's five brothers of their pending doom if they do not repent, Abraham's response was, "If they do not hear Moses and the Prophets, neither will they be persuaded though one rise from the dead" (See Luke 16:19-31).

The message is clear. Once the authority of God's word has been established, nothing more is needed. For us, if we reject the already-laid-down evidence authenticating the messianic life and death of Christ, then no modern-day miracle will serve any further purpose. However much we may cherish a personal miracle, we no longer have any need for miracles, signs and wonders. In fact, Jesus called out the Pharisees and Sadducees for their hypocrisy, failing to acknowledge the miracles already witnessed when they again asked for "a sign from heaven" to test Him. Jesus admonished them and squarely stated, "An evil and adulterous generation seeks after a sign, and no sign shall be given to it except the sign of the prophet Jonah" (Matt. 16:4).

This ought to be a warning to those of us who callously petition God for a sign to appease our every whim. Yes, pray for guidance and for the fortitude and integrity of character to know God's will based on His word, but do not ask for a sign. This is the wrong kind of test to put before our Lord. Sincere as it may appear on the surface, such testing maligns the purpose of miracles wrought by God, and no sign shall be given.

Miracles did also attract many insincere people who were seeking only physical healing, but physical healing was never the primary end. Also, we must not lose sight of the fact that many divine wonders did not persuade all observers. The Psalmist lamented the obstinate-minded Israelites who had witnessed countless miracles but, "In spite of this they still sinned, and did not believe in His wonderful works" (Ps. 78:32). In stark contrast, the wicked people of the great city Nineveh believed and repented in response to Jonah's warning from God of pending doom, despite not a single miracle being recorded (Jonah 3:5). Similarly John the baptizer, who performed no miracles (John 10:41) and was labeled the greatest of all the prophets (Matt. 11:11), heralded a message preparing the way for salvation, which the tax-gatherers and harlots believed, but the chief priests and elders of the Jewish people did not.

From this point we can glean that a secondary purpose of miracles was to expose the sincerity of men's hearts. This is lucidly demonstrated at the Feast of Dedication in Jerusalem where the Jews who had witnessed many of Jesus's miracles still doubted His messianic declaration. They asked, "How long do you keep us in doubt? If you are the Christ, tell us plainly" (John 10:24). "Jesus answered them, 'I told you and you do not believe. The works that I do in My Father's name, they bear witness of Me. But you do not believe, because you are not of My sheep'" (John 10:25-26). These men of insincere heart likely had witnessed thousands of Jesus's supernatural feats, and still they refused to accept these attestations of Christ's deity because of their own obtuse nature.

As Jesus often taught in various places, He made very clear the purpose of his signs and wonders. The words from Luke 5:24 give us the most straightforward declaration of this purpose when Jesus answered the malicious scribes and Pharisees, "in order that you may know that the Son of Man has authority on earth to forgive sins." This fact shows us that, while miracles were essential to confirm that Jesus was God present in the flesh and that His declared way of salvation was true, miracles were not guaranteed to have its intended effect on all people. God bestowed free will upon us all. The same would be true if miracles still occurred in modern times.

At other times, sincere but doubting people were convinced by a miracle that God was, in fact, communicating with them. Gideon was a brave soldier and a strong leader, and he was no fool. When the angel of the Lord appeared to him and said, "The Lord is with you, O valiant warrior," Gideon was having some serious doubts about this declaration. The Israelites in their wickedness were defeated by the Midianites and had been harshly oppressed for seven years. By now they were begging God for deliverance. Gideon candidly voiced his doubt to the angel and asked, "If the Lord is with us, why then has all this happened to us? And where are all His miracles which our fathers told us about?" (Judg. 6:13).

Can you just read Gideon's mind? "Yeah, right! Tell me another story. I need some proof here!" And that's just what he asked for: "Show me a sign that it is you who talk with me" (Judg. 6:17). The angel of the Lord performed a miracle, and then Gideon shouted, "Alas, O Lord God!" (Judg. 6:22) Despite this, Gideon still was hesitant about going against the Midianites, so he asked God for another test with the fleece (Judg. 6:39). We are then told the account of how the Midianites were defeated by Gideon's army.

In at least one setting, the "unbelievers" who were in need of a miraculous verification were actually Christians. Although throughout Scripture God declared how He would offer salvation to all mankind, the early church initially consisted only of Jewish converts. It was not until several years after the Church Age began that the first Gentiles were added to the church. In Acts 10 we read about the Roman household of Cornelius, a centurion, "a devout man and one who feared God with all his household" (v. 2), and to whom Peter shared the Gospel message. As Peter was prophesying to them, they began to "speak with tongues and magnify God" (v. 46). Observe that Paul told the Corinthian Christians that "tongues are for a sign, not to those who believe but to unbelievers; but prophesying is not for unbelievers but for those who believe" (1 Cor. 14:22). In the setting of Acts 10, Cornelius and his family were the believers—they strongly believed in God; and the Jewish Christians were the unbelievers, as they still had doubts about Gentiles being allowed into the Christian brotherhood. When the unbelieving Jewish Christians witnessed the miraculous sign of tongues spoken by Gentiles and saw that God was "giving them the Holy Spirit, just as He also did to us" (Acts 15:8), they believed. This miracle confirmed the message that God "made no distinction between us and them, purifying their hearts by faith" (Acts 15:9).

We are shown repeatedly that miracles are a sign or wonder performed to reveal God's will. Another serious area of confusion arises with regard to the perseverance of miracles beyond the apostolic age. If a miracle is defined as a supernatural event that occurs for the purpose of revealing and authenticating God's will, and if we now have a completed document of the Bible that is the sole source of knowing God's will, then what would be the purpose of modern-day miracles? Paul asserts in 2 Timothy 3:16-17 that "all Scripture is given by inspiration of God, and is profitable for doctrine, for reproof, for correction, for instruction in righteousness, that the man of God may be complete, thoroughly equipped for every good work." This implies that miracles are no longer necessary to authenticate God's message. All that is spoken of God, all preaching and teaching, comes from the Bible. Every teaching, we are told, should be tested against the Scriptures, the completed written text of the Bible.

Where then is the need for miracles? With proper exegesis, the answer to all our spiritual queries can be found in Scripture. All the miracles performed in the first century have already authenticated the Bible that we now have in its complete form, and we can trust in the genuineness and truth of God's written word because of that validation. Therefore, the miraculous validation of the Bible is no longer needed because the confirmatory work has already been done.

This discourse on the word *miracle* is not intended to stir the emotions or incite anger, but to demonstrate the importance of the meaning and purpose of a single word. Failing to recognize and accept the meaning and purpose of a word can ruinously divide a cohesive church body. Being unwilling to relinquish our allegiance to a modern-day status quo for the sake of popular but spurious religious thought is schismatic and unwarranted. Anyone who departs from a solid interpretation of Scripture becomes a tool of Satan to divide the body of Christ. Remember, the Lord hates "one who sows discord among the brethren" (Prov. 6:19b). Words have meaning, and that meaning should never be distorted or nullified. Somewhere along our spiritual journey, we all have been taught as true doctrine some things that do not coincide with what the Bible actually teaches. If we avow to accurately define the meaning and purpose of words, and to allow the Bible to speak for itself in proper context, then we are much better equipped to recognize and correct flawed doctrine and beliefs when they arise. A popular teaching is not necessarily a correct teaching.

The Law of Harmony

The law of harmony states that nothing in the Bible is contradictory. Many isolated topics are developed in the Bible, yet the composite truths of the Bible are never at odds with one another. While *apparent* contradictions may exist, valid and true contradictions are nowhere found in Scripture. All apparent contradictions are resolved by harmonizing parallel passages of Scripture on a given topic, and by paying close attention to immediate and surrounding context. When a specific command is given to a single individual in an isolated situation, this does not necessarily imply a universal principle. Many errors of interpretation result from falsely assuming that because God specifically instructed an individual (as recorded in Scripture), this same instruction must apply to us.

While every devout Christian ought to place a high priority on knowing God's will, we should never construe a unique command to a historical figure, for a specific purpose, as being an obligatory command to every Christian. Likewise, a promise. When the prophets and teachers at the Antioch church were ministering to the Lord, "the Holy Spirit said, 'Now separate to Me Barnabas and Saul for the work to which I have called them'" (Acts 13:2). When Luke the physician recorded this fact, God still spoke to the apostles and prophets in such ways. We should not assume that this form of communication still prevails today. We no longer have the apostles or any prophets directly communicating to us (No doubt some would argue this point, but this is the clear teaching of 2 Timothy 3:16-17). Thus, a harmony of Scripture is needed to ascertain what and how God communicates to us today. Rather than direct verbal communication from the Holy Spirit, we now have a finished written record of God's will for His people, inspired by the Holy Spirit, whereby we are now "complete, thoroughly equipped for every good work" (2 Tim. 3:17). We have indeed been "sealed with the Holy Spirit of promise" (Eph. 1:13), who now sanctifies us (Rom. 15:16). By harmonizing Scripture, we are able to "test the spirits, whether they are of God" (1 John 4:1).

The Bible is a compilation of many historical events that unfold as a revelation of God's plan of salvation for a sin-fallen world. We are given only one path to eternal life, not three or five. Every principle taught on Christian living can only be validated or corroborated by a perusal of different texts that address the same principle. One lesson cannot negate another, and each part contributes to the whole. Every passage of Scripture builds on another, and each of the sixty-six books of the Bible is an incomplete part of the whole message.

Every book serves a unique purpose and contributes to the full picture that God intended us to have so that we may know Him and know what He expects of us. Each sentence must be read in the context of sentences immediately before and after it, but also in the context of the whole chapter (which is an artificial designation for our own convenience, incidentally), and in the entire book.

The law of harmony means that no verse of Scripture stands alone or contradicts another verse. Every brick supporting the structure of Christian theology is necessary to complete the fullness of God's revelation of Himself to us. We see in the Bible a unity of purpose (redemption), a unity of perspective (God's) and a unity of teaching (righteousness) to guide us into holy living and the inheritance of eternal life. We must therefore remain sensitively aware of any teacher who renders interpretations that conflict with any solidly established principle elsewhere in the holy text. As a general rule of harmony, when an apparent contradiction exists, look for the defining principle and compare it to all similar (parallel) passages. We must never grieve the Holy Spirit by slothful and indiscriminate interpretation, lest unity be compromised.

Typology

In the course of God's progressive revelation of Himself and His redemptive plan throughout Scripture, we find historical events, persons, or things in the Old Testament that hold symbolic meaning in a prophetic way that would later be unfolded with its more profound and clear meaning in the New Testament. The original "type," or model, described in the Old Testament is compared to a richer fulfillment, the "antitype," in the New Testament. The corresponding antitypes of the New Testament are not arbitrary and should never be confabulated by the reader in order to impose his own interpretation on Old Testament records. As Ramm emphasizes by citing Bishop Marsh in his *Lectures on the Criticism and Interpretation of the Bible*, "a type is a type only if the New Testament specifically so designates it to be such."[7] While some scholars may consider this too strict a definition, the greater error is to assign a new revelation or meaning of an Old Testament type that is artificial or fabricated for the sake of novelty or convenience.

Antitypes are described and defined by the New Testament authors who render an apparent fuller meaning or a fulfillment of the corresponding type. We often see these in the context of the Tabernacle and in the Levitical priesthood, as compared to the heavenly tabernacle and the priesthood of all believers. Type-antitype constructs may include persons, events, places, things, offices or ceremonies. In Romans 5:14 Adam is described as "a type of Him who was to come," contrasting the transgression of one man Adam (that cursed all mankind with death) with "the gift by the grace of one Man, Jesus Christ," which resulted in a way of justification and redemption from that transgression.

Places such as the wilderness and the Promised Land typify searching for God and the heavenly home. Manna was given to sustain the life of the wandering Israelites in the wilderness, whose antitype is the "true bread from heaven" which "gives life to the world" (John 6:32-33). Typology shows us how God has acted in the affairs of mankind and specifically influenced events throughout the world's history. Typology also clarifies God's design for His creation and for the reconciliation of mankind. If we pay attention to these passages, we can learn much about how we ought to conduct our lives according to God's wondrous plan. On the other hand, should we choose to ignore the clear message of such passages, we will surely stumble in our own lives. The Bible is replete with types and antitypes. When we neglect the evident meaning of typological lessons, we are sure to confuse ourselves, and confusion always further divides the church.

One general area of such confusion arising from types and antitypes pertains to the old and new covenant itself. Jeremiah prophesied, "'Behold, days are coming,' declares the Lord, 'when I will make a new covenant with the house of Israel and with the house of Judah'" (Jer. 31:31). Those days have come to pass. The old covenant is finished, being fully replaced by the new covenant. We see the old Jerusalem compared with the new or heavenly Jerusalem. The new circumcision of the heart contrasts with the old circumcision of the flesh, and the old covenant is a thing of the past. Yes, it did serve its purpose, but the traditions and laws of the Old Testament could not save us, and they are now null and void. In Christ we see the fulfillment of the Law. This point is affirmed in Colossians 3:8-17, emphasizing "the new man who is renewed in knowledge [not by lineage], where there is neither Greek nor Jew, circumcised nor uncircumcised, barbarian, Scythian, slave nor free, but Christ is all and in all" (vv. 10-11).

As Christians, we must rightfully acknowledge that the Jews "were entrusted with the oracles of God" (Rom 3:2), but those oracles were a confirmation of our spiritual death apart from the saving blood of Jesus Christ. The Old Testament, full of rich history and many important life lessons, gives us no way of salvation. It only testifies that salvation is coming. The descendants of Abraham are no longer defined by a genealogic thread but by the saving blood of Christ. The old system of animal sacrifice was finished forever with the spilling of Jesus's blood on the cross. The temple of stone has yielded to the temple of the Holy Spirit.

Despite all this out-with-the-old, in-with-the-new typology, many Christians appear determined to restore the old, and this is seeking nothing less than a curse. It is a revival of the Galatian heresy, of seeking to return to the Law. We see this pervasively in the eschatology wars. While a discourse on dispensational theology is beyond the scope of this writing, dispensationalism teaches that Israel and the Christian Church are distinct entities. This theology demands a literal interpretation method, and requires a suspension of the rules of harmony and typology. Dispensationalism is itself divided into several different views. Let us not be so naïve as to believe that all views of the end times are acceptable. Each dispensational view results from an interpretation or a misinterpretation of what Scripture reveals about the events leading to the Day of Judgment. Each of these interpretations has its own consequences of effect in our daily Christian walk. What we consider inconsequential may or may not deeply affect our actions as Christians. Allow me to cite an example.

One group of premillenialists, called dispensationalists, regards the Christian Church and the nation of Israel as two distinct and enduring entities recognized by God. They hold to a literal Old Testament interpretation of the restoration of the nation Israel that will culminate with a rebuilding of the Jewish temple in Jerusalem.

Let's go no farther, but ask ourselves to think logically about this view in terms of typology, considering the Old and New covenants. If the old city of Jerusalem is restored, does that bequeath on Jews a special blessing from God? Shall they somehow secure salvation through their Jewish heritage, by resuming the practice of animal sacrifice in the temple? If so, then what is the meaning of Jesus's words in John 14:6, "I am the way, the truth and the life; no one comes to the Father, but through me"?

Shall we arbitrarily modify the words "no one" to mean "no one but the Jews"? If the Jews still fail to accept Jesus on His own terms as their Redeemer-Savior, then are they not spiritually lost and unregenerate? What did the apostle Peter mean when he preached to the Jewish leaders, "Nor is there salvation in any other, for there is no other name under heaven given among men by which we must be saved" (Acts 4:12)? Jesus called the unbelieving Jewish scribes and Pharisees "serpents, brood of viper!" and asked them, "How can you escape the condemnation of hell?" (Matt. 23:33). If "we have been sanctified through the offering of the body and blood of Jesus Christ once for all" (Heb. 10:10), then what would be the purpose of rebuilding of the Jewish temple? What end would a restoration of the sacrificial system serve, save to proclaim the sacred blood of Christ of no effect? It simply makes no sense to be anticipating a literal restoration of the Jewish temple to revive a system of animal sacrifice and the Law that only cursed us and could not save.

No, according to the clear teaching of the New Testament, all Jews must enter the new covenant with Christ as their Savior to attain to eternal life. There is no other way. Therefore, every Jew, now and forever, has set before him a choice between life and death in the same way that every other person must choose. If a Jew rejects the one and only way of salvation for mankind, he is destined for eternal damnation. This is clearly what the New Testament teaches. To ignore or distort the important teachings of typology is to jeopardize one's salvation, regardless of one's genealogy. If we as Christians were to not evangelize a practicing Jew, thinking them to be saved because of their genealogic affiliation, we have fostered their spiritual demise. This mutilation of typology has severely and unnecessarily partitioned the body of Christ.

Literal Versus Figurative

The greatest portion of Holy Scripture is written to be understood by a literal interpretation. The term literal means, "to be taken in the normal way." Much as we would read any novel or speak in the usual course of daily conversation, this is how most of Scripture should to be interpreted. The Bible ought to generally be read in the literal sense, unless the context itself specifically suggests a non-literal interpretation.

When a non-literal, or figurative, interpretation is necessary, such a position is actually derived and understood from the literal understanding of other texts. The decision to interpret literally or figuratively is often readily discerned by the genre, the literary form or style of the book. The Bible consists of various genres, including the Law, history, wisdom and poetry, prophecy, the Gospels, epistles (or letters), and apocalyptic writings. The books of the Law, historical books, and the letters as a rule are to be interpreted literally, although various figures of speech are also used in many of these books. These portions were not intended to be literally understood. In the Gospels, Jesus often spoke in such a way as to encrypt the meaning of His words from insincere hearers, such as when He spoke in parables. In apocalyptic writings such as Daniel and Revelation, the authors often spoke in highly symbolic language and used figures of speech, allegories or other nonliteral language to convey deeper meanings or truths, to highlight an important principle, to render a teaching more memorable, or possibly even to obscure specific and impertinent details.

When deciding on whether to interpret a passage literally or figuratively, we must pay careful attention to the context, literary style and intent of the author. The basic principles of hermeneutics must never be abandoned. If a word or statement makes sense as it stands, then a literal interpretation must be presumed. If a literal translation makes no sense, then we should seek a figurative interpretation.

In John 10:9 Jesus says, "I am the door." By reason of simple logic, we assume a figurative interpretation and seek the further meaning by looking at context. A little later (John 14:6), Jesus abandoned his figurative speech and plainly stated, "I am the way, the truth, and the life; no one comes to the Father, except through Me." When Jesus told the multitudes the parable of the wheat and tares in Matthew 13:24-30, He figuratively told how the good and bad seed were allowed to grow together until the harvest, at which time the tares (bad seed) would first be gathered up, bound and burned, and the wheat would be gathered into the barn. He later departed from the crowd of people and explained to His disciples the deeper meaning of the allegorical narrative, comparing the kingdom of heaven to a field containing both good and bad crops (Matt. 13:36-43). Interestingly, Jesus describes a sequence of first removing the wicked, and then glorifying the faithful, something quite contradictory to the modern belief of a "rapture" of the faithful before the Day of Judgment.

Sometimes we may be tempted to assign a figurative over a literal interpretation if a passage does not fit into our present theological schema. In the creation account of Genesis, we read that on the fifth day "God created the great sea creatures and every living thing that moves, with which the waters abounded, after their kind" (Gen. 1:21). What sort of images do the words "great sea creatures" conjure up in your mind? Many an ancient sailor has described various sorts of gigantic and fearsome creatures of the deep in sea lore. Perhaps you are thinking more in the realm of gargantuan whales or giant squid. After all, they exist in our modern world. Is this what the Genesis account describes?

On the sixth day of creation, "God made the beasts of the earth after their kind." Most people would consider these beasts to include the dinosaurs by evidence of their existence in the fossil record. Some scholars question whether or not a "creation day" was an actual twenty-four hour period of time or something more comparable to the Devonian Era, a figurative interpretation. But notice the rendition, "so the evening and the morning" were attributed to each of the six creation days. This evening and morning certainly suggests a *literal* day, but this would not allow for the eons of evolutionary progression necessary for an atheistic conception of the world that even some theologians feel compelled to integrate into the Bible construct of the Creation. Since nothing contained in the text suggests figurative language, a literal interpretation is most reasonable and suggests that all the species were present at the one instant of time in the creation process by the power of God's word. This is exactly what God's word in the Bible claims.

Taking this concept a little further, we must assume by evidence of the fossil record that when God created the great sea monsters and beasts of the earth, these included the dinosaurs. The largest of the dinosaurs are no longer walking the earth, but we do have skeletal remains of the likes of Tyrannosaurus Rex, Apatosaurus, and Plesiosaurus, the last being a sea-dwelling dinosaur. Their bony fossilized remains confirm they existed in the past. Indeed, we are given a detailed description of just such a creature as Apatosaurus in the book of Job, which is believed to be the earliest written book of the Bible.

In Job chapter 40, God is questioning the wisdom of Job regarding the power and wonders of His creation. In a discourse teaching Job a lesson in humility, God cites an abundance of phenomena present in the visible world in which Job lived. He describes the constellations, the mysteries of the sea currents and weather, the intricacies of animal behavior, all of which Job had no doubt observed but could not explain. Among these familiar observations of Job's world, God mentions "behemoth, which I made along with you" (Job 40:15ff). This giant land animal is described as "the first of the ways of God," a grazer whose "strength is in his hips, and his power is in his stomach muscles. He moves his tail like a cedar; the sinews of his thighs are tightly knit. His bones are like beams of bronze, his ribs like bars of iron." This animal was so huge that "indeed the river may rage, yet he is not disturbed."

God's implication to Job is, "Would anyone dare to tangle with this creature?" Given this magnificent description, how could this creature possibly be defined as "the hippopotamus" as so rendered in *Eerdmans' Handbook to the Bible*?[8] This reference work rightly assigns a literal interpretation to the passage, but errs in attributing this description to the likes of a hippopotamus. Have you ever seen the tail of a hippo? It sways its tail more like a little fly swatter, anything but "like a cedar." This is a fine work of scholarly eisegesis, providing not even close to an accurate interpretation of "the first of the ways of God" (Gen. 40:19). The creature described in Job chapter 40 does fit that of an Apatosaurus or other similar titanosaur.[9]

Theologians do no better when defining "Leviathan" as a crocodile.[10] Job 41 describes a creature having all the features of a ferocious, fire-breathing dragon. Could this possibly have been one of the great sea monsters described in Genesis 1:21? Since this description is given right along with other animals described in the natural world of Job's time, we have every reason to assign a literal interpretation to this fearsome creature of the sea.

The most common error committed by Christians reading this passage is that of disbelief. The dragon certainly was no creature fabricated in the lore of eastern mythology but obviously belonged to the family of "great sea creatures" created by God as described in the Genesis history. A fire-breathing dragon is not at all beyond the imagination of any rational comparative zoologist. One needs only to conceive of an organic source of fuel and a way to ignite it. We know that methanogenic (methane gas-producing) bacteria residing in the anaerobic environment of animal intestinal tracts produce methane or natural gas. If this gas was belched up and ignited by a spark-generating organ in the throat of a sea creature, such as a charge created by an electric eel, Voilà! You might ask why haven't the remains of these dragons been found in the fossil record? Well, they likely *have* been discovered. The soft tissues of the digestive tract would have rapidly decayed, leaving no fossil remains, but we do have fossilized bones of Plesiosaurus as a candidate dragon. Perhaps stories like *Puff the Magic Dragon* have contributed to the mythologizing of dragons, but the Bible says this creature existed in Job's time. Whenever a literal interpretation makes sense or is demanded from the context, we ought to take the passage literally, and not necessarily try to fit it into our modern world. Remember: strive for exegesis rather than eisegesis.

Other symbolic passages of Scripture plainly demand a figurative interpretation. The vivid apocalyptic imagery found in Ezekiel, Daniel, and Revelation have wrought havoc in many churches because some undisciplined interpreters have formulated their own imaginative stories of what all the symbols and metaphors mean. How many times have doomsday prophets wrongly declared a precise date for the end of the world? We have at our fingertips an abundance of websites to tickle our fancy with predictions of the coming Mark of the Beast, a new world order, World War Three, the cashless world bank, detailed rapture predictions, and other end times propaganda.

Viewing an extensive list of historical dates predicting apocalyptic events is entertaining, to say the least. Wikipedia lists 173 past predictions and seven future predictions for the end of the world.[11] Past prognosticators have come from a wide variety of sources, including Martin Luther, Christopher Columbus, Cotton Mather, John Wesley, Charles Taze Russell, Herbert W. Armstrong, Jehovah's Witnesses, Jean Dixon, Charles Manson, Pat Robertson, Nostradamus, Jerry Falwell, Tim LaHaye, and a host of others.

Since their prophecies did not come to pass, all of these people or groups must be declared false prophets, by the Bible's own definition. They have misrepresented God's word, and this is a serious offense. Sadly, false prophecies will continue to the very end when Christ actually does return. We should have no affirming or enabling fellowship with all such unfaithful workers, however popular or esteemed they may be. Remember, Jesus never once displayed a crowd-pleaser mentality, and He repeatedly warns us to beware of false teachers. Following purveyors of fanciful claims is hazardous to our spiritual health.

Nowhere else must we diligently practice the discipline of good apologetics than when interpreting highly symbolic literature. A diligent study of Bible symbols and figures of speech, of which there are many hundreds, is a necessary prerequisite if we are to do justice to interpreting these apocalyptic books. Even the most devout and advanced scholar must occasionally concede to ignorance rather than risk misinterpretation. We must never ignore the grave warnings and consequences of misrepresenting God's testimony given us in the closing words of the Bible (Rev. 22:18-19).

Cultural Versus Normative

Tremendous confusion may arise when an action, principle, teaching or precedent is not contextually and historically discerned. Cultural instructions pertained to past times only, and normative teachings are meant to stand as guiding principles for all time. Some practices in ancient days had a practical application that would be meaningless today. Foot washing, for example, was a normal part of hospitality because travelers walked on dusty roads. Wearing sandals, their feet got dirty, and a foot-washing basin was likely a standard utensil of the home. Washing the feet was a cultural practice that demonstrated cordiality to visitors. Paul mentions washing of the feet as a genial practice of a widow worthy of honor and support (1 Tim. 5:10).

Jesus, on the other hand, used this cultural practice to teach by example a great principle to His disciples, that a slave or servant is not greater than his master, and that humility must be a way of life as an expression of true godliness. While foot washing was very much a part of that culture, the principle as an example of humility has application for all time. The foot-washing practice was cultural, but the principle is normative.

Many women (and men) who read 1 Timothy 2:11-12 regarding a woman's demeanor in public worship take offense at this passage because they do not understand the gender roles established by God's beautiful design. Many attempts have been made to declare this passage a cultural practice, giving plausible reasons for their viewpoint, and thereby tacitly apologizing for Paul's "bold assertions." Some Christian leaders—and I have heard this firsthand— have labeled Paul a chauvinist and a misogynist. Paul, however, makes very clear that this principle of a woman quietly receiving instruction with entire submissiveness is a normative principle, meaning one that is intended to apply for all time. We know this because Paul appeals to the creation of Adam and Eve to justify this teaching. Paul is not just dealing with a practical matter in corporate worship but is putting forth a normative theological principal that has bearing on more than public worship. (See also 1 Cor. 14:34-37.) Otherwise he would not have cited the creation order as a basis for his assertion.

Alexander Strauch describes another biblical teaching that grates on the nerves of some who do not accept the normative principle of a male leadership model in the New Testament churches. In his book *Biblical Eldership*, he drives home the point of headship and submission by God's divine order when he states, "It is profoundly significant that God did not create Adam and Eve at the same time. Instead, woman was made after the man, from the man, for the man, brought to the man, and named by the man (Gen. 2:20-23; cf. 1 Cor. 11:8,9)."[12] He rightly demonstrates that God's design of man and woman instills deep within our fabric the roles for which both men and women are innately constructed. Nothing in God's design is demeaning or harmful. Both men and women may abuse their roles, and only the abuse of these roles leads to strife. To refute this natural order of God is to rebel against the Creator Himself. Dare we arrogantly claim that we know better than He? Male eldership is a normative principle. The husband as head of the family is normative, but a servant headship as Jesus taught is also normative. The domineering husband who does not love his wife as Christ loves the church is not in God's grace. He is no less than a tyrant. When we read and heed God's design for His creation, good things result.

In contrast to this endearing principle, when Moses described the rendering of the sacrificial lamb for the Jewish Passover feast (Exodus 12), he was giving specific instructions for a feast to commemorate the Lord's tenth plague on the Egyptians and the "passing over" of the Israelites' first born. Since the Passover celebration is no longer required under the New Covenant, these instructions are culturally relative but have no abiding influence on us today.

Male circumcision is another such example. The error of trying to impose a normative role on a cultural practice such as an ancient feast or male circumcision is poor scholarship. So also is the mistake of ignoring universal principles simply because we find them culturally distasteful due to a modern secular influence borne out of earthly wisdom. Once again, we see how poor interpretive skills lead to strife and division in the church.

Nearest Antecedent Rule

This rule declares that a modifying pronoun (he/she, they/them, you, it) or a demonstrative adjective (this/these, that/those) refers back to the nearest noun that appears in the context, unless the context clearly necessitates a more distant qualifier. The wily Bible interpreter misuses this rule with great liberty to deceive the weak and gullible believer, resulting in tragic consequences.

Jesus stated in Luke 10: 8-9, "and whatever city you enter, and they receive you, eat what is set before you; and heal those who are sick…." Jesus conferred this ability to heal the sick on the "you" in this passage. The nearest antecedent rule necessitates that "you" refers back to the "seventy others" and not to all Christians.

When the apostle John states in his first letter, "These things I have written to you" (1 John 5:13), the "you" logically refers back to "My little children" cited in 1 John 2:1, but the recipient of "these things" is also specifically mentioned in the same verse (13), namely, "you who believe in the name of the Son of God." Correctly applying the nearest antecedent rule maintains the integrity of a passage by accurately certifying what corresponds to whom. We must not assume that every time we read the word "you" it refers to you the reader. Many errors are made by such careless interpretation.

Law of Parsimony

Parsimony is a scientific principle declaring that the simplest explanation for a scientific observation is usually the correct one. In Bible interpretation, the parsimony rule states that, for any passage in the Bible, the simplest explanation of the text is to be preferred over a more complex reasoning, unless clearly warranted by other supportive passages.

Here is a straightforward secular example. If I awakened in the morning and observed my pasture to be soaked and concluded, "It must have rained last night," rather than speculate, "The neighbors must have come and hosed down my pasture last night," then I would be applying the law of parsimony. This law is often violated by theologians who are motivated to defend otherwise untenable positions, aspiring to denominational loyalty over a quest for a less favorable but evident biblical truth. A cultist who wishes to lay claim on an Old Testament principle may quote Hebrews 13:8, "Jesus Christ is the same yesterday, today, and forever," but the parsimony principle means that God is immutable by nature, not that what God demanded in the past is always demanded in the present. (Otherwise, why would He have introduced a new covenant?) Jesus is omnipresent and omniscient by His nature, but he took on human form to bring us a new covenant to replace the old. Things have changed; He has not. Adherence to the law of parsimony keeps the Christ-centered scholar honest in his Bible search for meaning and truth.

Other Rules of Interpretation

Many other rules of sound interpretation exist and are worthy of study. I have not discussed in any great detail principles such as progressive revelation, figures of speech, specific literary genres, allegory, symbolism, parallels, doubling, epigrams, etymology, prophecy, and many other tenets of good interpretation. The reader is strongly encouraged to study further the correct usage of biblical language to be better equipped to honor God by respecting His words and interpreting them soundly. Also, a study of the New Testament Greek is invaluable in gaining deeper insights into the unfathomable riches therein. Many novel English versions have been written and take unnecessary liberties in translation that distort meaning. For this reason, much preferred for study are the more literal translations. While we have no perfect translations, some are much more accurate than others.

As we have seen, the crisis of disunity in the universal Christian church began at its inception and continues to torrentially plague the bride of Christ. But all of these schismatic devices have their roots in a flawed interpretation of Scripture. For this reason, we must always strive to get back to our origin, the Bible. We are a people of the Book. Our standard of faith, our sayings, and our doing of spiritual things must always derive from an accurate and unbiased rendering of Scripture. Unless we learn and understand sound interpretive principles and apply them diligently and in genuine humility of heart, without compromise, we are doomed to be instruments of division in the church. Rather than gather together the brotherhood, we scatter them abroad. If only one person in a local church dares to contend for God's truth based on what the Bible really teaches, that person becomes an agent of peace and unity, a true ambassador of Christ who represents our Lord with honor. May we all forever rejoice in the truth of God's uncompromised word.

Endnotes

1 A. Berkeley Mickelsen, *Interpreting the Bible*, Eerdmans, Grand Rapids, 1976 p. 113.

2 Bernard Ramm, *Protestant Biblical Interpretation*, 3rd ed., Baker Book House, Grand Rapids, 1970, p. 5.

3 Ibid.

4 William Strunk, Jr. and E. B. White, *The Elements of Style*, 50th Anniversary ed., Pearson, New York, 2009, p. xv.

5 W. E. Vine, "Vine's Expository Dictionary of NT Words," 2001-2019, <StudyLight.org>, accessed on April 12, 2019.

6 A. Depke, "baptizō," *Theological Dictionary of the New Testament*, Eerdmans, Grand Rapids, 1985, p. 92.

7 Bernard Ramm, Protestant Biblical Interpretation, 3rd ed., Baker Book House, Grand Rapids, 1970, p. 219.

8 David Alexander and Patricia Alexander (eds.), *Eerdmans' Handbook to the Bible*, Eerdmans, Grand Rapids, 1973, p. 326.

9 New archaeological findings have described various herbivorous land dinosaurs such as Argentinosaurus and Patagotitan, but the biblical description of behemoth describes a magnificently huge, herbivorous land-dwelling dinosaur, not a mere hippopotamus.

10 David Alexander and Patricia Alexander (eds.), *Eerdmans' Handbook to the Bible*, Eerdmans, Grand Rapids, 1973, p. 326.

11 "List of dates predicted for apocalyptic events," <http://www.en.m.wikipedia.org>, accessed on March 24, 2019.

12 Alexander Strauch, *Biblical Eldership*, Lewis and Roth, Littleton, CO, 1995, p. 60.

Chapter 10

Test Your Interpretive Skills

Any Christian possessing an ounce of humility would likely confess that he or she is at least somewhat limited in Bible knowledge and interpretive skill. Certainly, omniscience belongs to God alone. However, while we may be willing to give token admission to our weaknesses, on a more subconscious level we may esteem ourselves too grounded in the faith to be seriously challenged or questioned regarding our own spiritual beliefs or command of Scripture. I speak here to the theologian, to the church leader, to the preacher, to the life-long Christian.

Despite all we think we might know, we may greatly benefit from a glimpse into the looking glass now and then to ask ourselves, do we really know the Bible? Dare each of us ask, how strong is my understanding of Bible truth? How confident am I that I have not been misled in my knowledge of God's revelation to me? Perchance, have I possibly missed out on some fundamental teachings in the Bible? How many verses of Scripture might I have read a thousand times while completely missing their meaning? Do I still maintain a belief solely because my favorite teacher or seminary professor endorsed it?

Many of you reading this book may have been Christians for the longest part of your life, some sixty, seventy or more years.

You may have listened to thousands of sermons and maybe even faithfully devoted yourself to daily Bible reading for years. Perhaps you've gotten comfortable with your grasp of the Bible and assume you've heard most of what there is to be said about the Bible. When was the last time you heard anything different in a sermon, something that you have not already heard before? You might think you have it all down. That's great, because it means you have not ignored the word of God, and hopefully your diligence in examining God's word has translated into some real spiritual fruit in your life. God willing, it has yielded much good. But this familiarity may also breed complacency—a very dangerous and often costly state of mind.

A mere six months after the Japanese victory at Pearl Harbor, Japan suffered a horrific defeat from which they never recovered. Mitsuo Fuchida, the pilot who led the attack on Pearl Harbor, acknowledged in his book, *Midway: The Battle that Doomed Japan*, the primary reason for their defeat was they had become complacent. After Pearl Harbor, a sequence of subsequent careless command decisions rendered them vulnerable; then came their unexpected defeat.[1] Pride may go before a fall, but complacency is pride's greatest accomplice.

The dangerous pilot is not the young and inexperienced pilot, but the seasoned pilot having over ten thousand hours of flying time under his belt, and for whom flying has become mundane. In aviation, complacency is deadly. The aviator who thinks he knows it all, has seen and done it all, is most at risk of becoming the next aircraft casualty. So it is when we've been sitting on our pious haunches for too long. Sometimes we need a wakeup call.

James tells us in his epistle, "But be doers of the word, and not hearers only, deceiving yourselves" (Jas. 1:22), reminding us that the effectual doer "will be blessed in what he does" (Jas. 1:25). This should strongly motivate us toward ensuring that we are "hearing" the word accurately and in all its fullness. Faithful obedience is a product of faithful interpretation. If we are hearing the wrong message, where is the obedience? People also tend to hear only what they want to hear, and see only what appeals to their mind's eye.

We naturally harbor a strong affinity for the "convenient truth" that comforts and bolsters our presently held assertions. This faulty hearing and seeing is indeed a form of complacency, an intellectual and spiritual laziness. Selective hearing and vision can also be a form of cowardice. We are naturally inclined to veer away from uncomfortable Scripture passages that don't fit well into our working model of faith, preferring the path of least resistance. We may opt to respect our denominational boundaries, falsely equating loyalty to sect with loyalty to God. This mode of thinking is spiritually dangerous.

The veteran pilot averts such complacency by career-long flight simulator training where he is challenged with new and difficult situations that continually force him out of his comfort zone. In this "hostile" environment, he is confronted with every conceivable inflight emergency. By facing his worst fears in a controlled environment, he becomes more confident and able to accept and skillfully handle the unforeseen real-world challenges that someday may be forced upon him in flight. Christians would likewise gain much from similar training in discerning biblical truth. While truth never changes, our perception and grasp of truth should heighten as we mature and age.

In that vein, would you be willing to accept a little testing of your Bible knowledge? Will you submit to a challenge that may both test and sharpen your interpretive skills? The purpose of this chapter is not to trip you up or induce any feelings of inadequacy in your Bible knowledge. It is not intended to confound or discredit any specific denominational belief. It is simply to make you think. If perhaps you find yourself holding any wrong beliefs, don't feel too bad. It doesn't necessarily mean you're a heretic. On the other hand, be discerning. Sure, even I could mislead you. But let's agree beforehand to just let the Bible speak to us plainly. Hopefully it will render you more critically discerning as you read the Scriptures, since that is the ultimate goal.

An Itsy-bitsy Little Test

Before we get to the Bible, which admittedly can be a challenge to interpret, how about if we first test ourselves by interpreting a simple story, say, a nursery rhyme. Nearly everyone has heard the sonnet *Mary Had a Little Lamb*. Here's the first stanza:

> Mary had a little lamb,
> Its fleece was white as snow.
> And everywhere that Mary went
> The lamb was sure to go.

Applying the rules of sound interpretation to a nursery rhyme ought to be quite simple. Based solely on the above stanza, and in the interest of making this really easy, let me ask you to take a straightforward true or false quiz about its content.

Mary was a young girl	T	F
Mary also had a goat and a pig	T	F
Mary had a great big lamb	T	F
The lamb was always with Mary	T	F
The lamb obviously loved Mary	T	F

How many answers did you score as true? How many false? Actually, none of the statements can be answered either true of false. The stanza says nothing about Mary's age. It makes no mention about her having any other farm animals, including possibly a larger lamb. It is unlikely that the lamb followed Mary into the house, or into the bathroom or up into a tree house. We have no idea of the lamb's affections for Mary. She may have dragged the unwilling animal around on a tight leash that tormented the poor little animal, for all we know.

None of the above statements can be answered unless we are given more information. Now, I would not be at all surprised if some literalists among you are ready to argue my point. After all, the rhyme states very clearly, *"Everywhere* that Mary went, the lamb was sure to go." Everywhere means everywhere, right? Yes, but if Mary had a tree house accessed by a makeshift ladder of boards nailed to the tree, given the physical limitations of sheep, the lamb would be unable to climb this ladder. If Mary went to see her dentist, how likely would it be that he would allow a lamb into his office? Would Mary's mother allow the lamb to bathe in the tub with her? (Or was Mary a mother herself?) A hard-core literalist may still take exception to my claim that none of the statements can be declared absolutely true or false. At this point, we may face a fractioning of the Mary's Little Lamb Club. Okay then, for the sake of unity, let's allow all to believe whatever they wish. After all, our eternal souls are not in jeopardy here.

A Not So Itsy-bitsy Little Test

When interpreting the Bible, the stakes are higher. This is not to say that every misinterpretation of Scripture is damning, or that incomplete knowledge renders our hearts less pure. Instead, what accurate interpretation of the Scriptures does is protect us from the many false teachers in the world, and often in the churches. A right interpretation is foundational to a right understanding, equipping us in "teaching them to observe all that I commanded you," as Jesus commissioned his disciples to do (Matt. 28:20).

What now follows is another drill, this time in rightly discerning God's word. The format is simple. I'll just ask ten questions and then give a straightforward referenced biblical answer to each question. Many of you will no doubt answer by recalling what you have been taught, but you may be surprised by what you thought you knew. I have chosen some topics that are for the most part non-threatening to most Christians' fundamental beliefs, but will also challenge you to look further into those beliefs that you cherish as heirlooms of your own faith. Remember that our goal is always to seek God's truths, not man's myths. Let's begin.

10 Questions

1. What was the first plague inflicted on an Egyptian pharaoh?
2. Could Jesus Himself, being the Son of God, be filled with the Holy Spirit?
3. How many gifts did the magi (wise men) bring to Jesus?
4. The Death Angel killed the Egyptian firstborn, both of people and animals. True or false?
5. How many apostles of Christ were there?
6. Which of the apostles doubted a resurrected Jesus?
7. Who is the oldest man who ever lived?
8. Why did God command Adam and Eve not to touch the fruit of the tree of knowledge of good and evil?
9. Where did Saul's conversion take place?
10. What persons were present to witness the birth of Jesus?

10 Answers

1. The first account of any plagues committed against an Egyptian pharaoh is recorded in Genesis 12:17. "The Lord struck Pharaoh with great plagues because of Sarai, Abram's wife." Because we are given no details as to the nature of these plagues, we have no idea what was the first plague. It was not turning the waters of the Nile to blood, which happened many years later.

2. Yes. Luke 4:1 states, "And Jesus, full of the Holy Spirit, returned from the Jordan and was led about by the Spirit in the wilderness."

3. We are not told how many gifts the wise men brought to Jesus. We are only informed, "they came in the house and saw the Child with Mary His mother; and they fell down and worshiped Him; and opening their treasures they presented to Him gifts of gold and frankincense and myrrh." We are not told how many gifts they brought, just that they brought gifts belonging to three categories. Did those treasures include many articles of gold? Probably so. And how many jars of frankincense and myrrh were brought will never be known this side of heaven.

4. Every verse of Scripture relating the event of the tenth plaque against Pharaoh reports that the Lord Himself killed the firstborn of the Egyptians as a final persuasion to cause Pharaoh to let the Israelites leave Egypt to worship their God. None of the passages mention anything about a "death angel." These verses include Exodus 11:1-6; 12:12, 13, 23, 27, 29; 13:15; Numbers 33:4; and Psalm 135:8. Exodus 12:23 mentions "the destroyer" but says nothing of a death angel. In this same verse we read, "For the Lord will pass through to smite the Egyptians, and when He sees the blood on the lintel and on the two doorposts, the Lord will pass over the door and will not allow the destroyer to come in to your houses to smite you." This "destroyer" may have been a lethal virus or bacteria, or some other infectious agent, but we are repeatedly told that the death sentence was carried out by the Lord, not by an angel.

5. The official number of apostles whom Jesus specifically called to follow Him at the outset of His earthly ministry is twelve (Luke 6:12-16). After Judas Iscariot hung himself, Matthias was chosen to replace him (Acts 1:26). A

few years later, along came Paul who claimed his apostleship by the will of Christ (Gal. 1:1). That makes fourteen apostles. The Greek word apostle (apóstolos) literally means "one who is sent forth." In a more general sense, Barnabas, Mark, Timothy, Titus, and all who were commissioned to carry out a specific mission were apostles. In his closing words in Romans 16, Paul sends a greeting to "Andronicus and Junias, my kinsmen, and my fellow prisoners, who are outstanding among the apostles, who also were in Christ before me." Some interpret this passage as meaning that they were Jesus's apostles, but the passage more likely implies (Context is king!) that they were well known to and highly regarded by the apostles. They themselves were not declared apostles, according to the formal requirements mentioned in Acts 1:21-22 for the selection of a replacement for Judas Iscariot.

6. Unfortunately, the apostle Thomas, who was absent the time Jesus first appeared to the other disciples receives a bad rap for refusing to believe without hard evidence that Jesus was truly resurrected. The phrase "doubting Thomas" was coined due to a failure in harmonizing Scripture. Recall in John's Gospel account that "when the doors were shut where the disciples were assembled, for fear of the Jews, Jesus came and stood in the midst, and said to them, 'Peace be with you.' When He had said this, He showed them His hands and His side. Then the disciples were glad when they saw the Lord" (John 20:19-20). This passage suggests that these disciples "were glad" *after* and *because* they saw the same evidence Thomas was demanding before he would believe. John 20:24 relates that Thomas "was not with them when Jesus came." Had the other disciples not been offered the evidence of Jesus's wounds, would they also have doubted? Yes. In fact, Matthew records

another version of Jesus appearing to the eleven disciples, and "when they saw Him, they worshipped Him; but some doubted" (Matt. 28:17). Mark 16:11 states that when Mary Magdalene told the disciples that Jesus was risen, "they did not believe." Read also verses 13 and 14. Some may argue that these words are written in a disputed text of the Bible, but Luke records the same account describing the women who "returned from the tomb and told all these things to the eleven and to all the rest" (Luke 24:9). Luke further details the event by stating, "It was Mary Magdalene, Joanna, Mary the mother of James; and the other women with them, who told these things to the apostles. And their words seemed to them like idle tales, and they did not believe" (Luke 24:10,11). Thus, *all* of the apostles doubted the risen Christ until they saw physical proof.

7. In Genesis 5:27 we are told, "So all the days of Methuselah were nine hundred and sixty-nine years, and he died." Many mistakenly declare Methuselah to be the oldest man who ever lived. This, of course, is presumptuous and is adding to the text something that is not stated. In truth, we have no idea who was the oldest human being who ever lived because to have that information we would have to know the age of everyone who ever died. All we can be sure of from the Bible verse is that Methuselah was the oldest living man *on record*. It says nothing about him being the oldest man who ever lived.

8. Adam was never given the command by God to not touch the fruit of the tree of knowledge of good and evil. Some mistakenly believe that the fall began as soon as Eve first touched the fruit. Genesis 3:1-6 records the temptation of Eve by the crafty serpent who asked Eve, "Has God indeed said, 'You shall not eat of every tree of the garden'?" (v.1). The question was very simple and straightforward, but the

bait was set for Eve. Pay close attention to her response. "And the woman said to the serpent, 'We may eat the fruit of the trees of the garden, but of the fruit of the tree which is in the midst of the garden, God has said, 'You shall not eat from it or touch it, lest you die''" (vv. 2,3). Eve's statement was distorted (The first example of eisegesis). God said nothing about touching the fruit. Rather, "And the Lord God commanded the man, saying, 'Of every tree of the garden you may freely eat; but of the tree of the knowledge of good and evil you shall not eat, for in the day that you eat of it you shall surely die'" (Gen. 2:16-17). God said nothing about *touching* the fruit. Adam and Eve could have touched the fruit all day long. They could have built a tree fort in the tree of life and plucked its fruit to throw around the garden for sport. They still would not have violated God's command to not *eat* of the fruit. This historical account of the fall of mankind shows us the cunning of Satan, how he can feed us truth and then confuse the issue before striking us down with a temptation. It is also worth noting that he questioned the word of God, then Eve answered by adding to the word of God. Dare we question God's words? Dare we allow anyone to change anything that God has commanded us to do or refrain from doing? This passage shows us not only how important obedience to God is, but also how carefully we must discern the actual words communicated by God.

9. Many Christians believe that Saul was converted by Jesus Himself on the road leading to Damascus. He was not. Saul's conversion from a relentless persecutor of those belonging to the Way to a staunch defender of the Christian faith is told in the ninth chapter of Acts. It occurred about three years after Jesus ended his earthly ministry. Jesus did grab Saul's attention as he was en route to Damascus by

flashing a blinding light from heaven that caused Saul to fall to the ground. By a voice only, not a visual appearance (called a theophany), Jesus asked, "Saul, Saul, why are you persecuting Me?" (v. 4). He then answers Saul's query to identify Himself by saying, "I am Jesus, whom you are persecuting" (v. 5). Jesus did not share the Gospel message with Saul. He simply gave Saul instructions (v. 6) to "arise and go into the city, and you will be told what you must do." Saul's conversion to Christianity occurred not on the road to Damascus but on a street called Straight at the house of Judas, in response to the Gospel message proclaimed to him by Ananias. Every conversion since Pentecost has resulted from a human agent proclaiming that same wonderful message.[2]

10. If you go into any department store during the Christmas season you are likely to see on display a variety of beautifully arranged snow-covered manger scenes, complete with the Holy family, two shepherds, three wise men, some sheep and a cow, and a manger filled with straw. Maybe a star shines brightly above the scene. This imagery tends to instill in us the belief that these figures were all present at the time of Jesus's birth, at the end of December. But what does the Bible say? The only details of Christ's birth are given in chapter two of Luke's Gospel. Mary accompanied Joseph to Bethlehem for a census decreed by Caesar Augustus. Since there was no room for them in a lodging place in that city, Mary birthed Jesus presumably in an animal stall since she wrapped him in cloths and laid Him in a feeding trough. Luke 2:7, and this verse alone, gives us all the details we know of the actual birth of Christ: "And she brought forth her firstborn Son, and wrapped Him in swaddling cloths, and laid Him in a manger, because there was no room for them in the inn." We are given no word of

who was actually present at His birth, or the exact location in Bethlehem where Jesus was born. Jewish custom would suggest that Mary was likely supported in childbirth by a midwife, as the husband would participate in the delivery only by exception, in an emergent or precipitous delivery. We know that Joseph was nearby since he was present when the shepherds arrived a short time later, but he was not necessarily present for the actual birth. Other female attendants may also have been there to support Mary. The shepherds were not in attendance because the angel of the Lord announced to them "for there is born to you this day in the city of David a Savior" (Luke 2:11). In verse 12, the angel also announced to the shepherds, "You will find a Babe wrapped in swaddling cloths, lying in a manger." The birth had already taken place at the time of this announcement. Since the shepherds were "in the same country" (v. 8) and "came with haste and found Mary and Joseph, and the Babe lying in a manger" (v. 16), we know that they were present shortly after Jesus's birth, but not at His birth. The wise men (or magi) came later, having traveled some distance from the east after they saw His star. They first came to Jerusalem and asked Herod where they might find Him, "He who has been born King of the Jews" (Matt. 2:2). Herod then "secretly called the wise men, determined from them what time the star appeared" (Matt. 2:7), and he later ordered the slaughter of "all the male children who were in Bethlehem and in all its districts, from two years old and under, according to the time which he had determined from the wise men" (Matt. 2:16). We deduce from this account that Jesus was likely at least a year old, but certainly under two years of age when the wise men arrived.

Avoid Erroneous Theology

So, as you can see, some things accepted as common knowledge about the Bible are not necessarily based on true facts. Any legend propagated for a long enough period of time tends to become accepted as an historical fact. The same is true of the Bible. While the details in these questions are not consequential for eternity, when critical teachings of Scripture are distorted, serious consequences may arise.

The intent of this exercise was not to frustrate, confound or overwhelm the reader. Its whole purpose was to show the importance of rightly discerning God's word so we can attain to an accurate rendering of what is written, and to be certain of what is not recorded. When we perpetuate teachings or ideas presumed but not known with biblical certainty, we submit ourselves to an "I think theology," and this always leads to confusion and division.

False teachings easily arise from false understandings, and these often become false tests of Christian fellowship. If some confusion or misunderstandings arose from the seemingly inconsequential issues raised by these ten questions, what other weightier doctrinal issues might likewise be obscured by mistaken theology and false understandings? And what impact on the body of Christ could this bear if Christians dogmatically hold to their false beliefs? Hopefully this little exercise will cause you to dig a little deeper into the Bible, to read it with more discernment, and to apply true logic and sound principles of interpretation when reading the word of God.

Endnotes

[1] Masatake Okumiya, and Mitsuo Fuchida, *Midway: The Battle That Doomed Japan*, Random House, New York, 1986. On a side note, following the war, Fuchida became a Christian evangelist to his own people.

[2] Many commentaries suggest that Saul's conversion was a miraculous event that occurred on the Damascus road, but the only miracle that took place was Jesus's plague of blindness on Saul that forced upon Saul an opportunity to soften his heart, preparing him to listen to the gospel message that was to be spoken by Ananias.

Chapter 11
Principles for Unity

As I stated at the beginning of this book, a universal oneness of the Christian church body is highly improbable because of the sinful nature of man, and because the evil forces in the spiritual realm have not yet been squelched. The crafty serpent is still at work in the world to confound seekers of righteousness. The high improbability of achieving a fully unified church should not at all dampen *the pursuit* of a like-minded church body. A faithful and true ambassador of Jesus Christ holds a higher office than any stately ambassador to a foreign country. The spokesperson for Jesus has a profound responsibility to faithfully represent with the greatest care and in full earnestness the agenda of the One to whom he or she pledges allegiance. We must always strive to do our best to bear a true message of salvation to the world, and to make disciples who are likewise loyal and true in their words and actions. Of course, the making of a true disciple begins with a fear and love of God in the evangelists' own hearts. If we do not genuinely love the Lord and are not called according to *His* purpose, then none of our actions will lead to any good in the quest for Christian unity.

This is not to imply that our imperfect faith and devotion to Jesus will be unfruitful if we at least try to be a true ambassador of peace and truth for a unified church. Like knights who zealously

209

embark on a conquest, if we are to have any hope of success, our mission for unity demands that we take some time to master a few simple principles in order to yield much fruit. The most important principle is a sound interpretation of God's message. Here are a few others.

Know the Word

The first principle to be understood in our pursuit of unity is that ignorance of God's word is not bliss. To be sure, we all possess limited and imperfect knowledge when it comes to knowing God's ways and His written word. No one has perfect discernment. Being flawed human beings, we will always struggle to fully understand and practice all things in Scripture. But that doesn't mean we should stop trying. We must never shirk our responsibility to remain faithful to God's word.

When Jesus prayed to His Father for His disciples in John 17, He emphasized the prime importance of faithfulness to God's word. "They were Yours, You gave them to Me, and they have kept Your word" (v. 6). "For I have given to them the words which You have given Me; and they have received them" (v. 8). "I have given them Your word" (v. 14). "Sanctify them by Your truth. Your word is truth" (v. 17). "I do not pray for these alone, but also for those who will believe in Me through their word; that they all may be one" (vv. 20-21).

If we are sanctified by the word of God, and if His word is truth, then what curse will befall those who willfully nullify, negate, distort, change, abbreviate, dilute, camouflage or eliminate any aspect of God's truth! The faithful ambassador for Christ must of first priority give heed to God's word. This means to know, to teach, and to obey God's word exactly as it is written.

Nobody has the right to change the content, the purpose, the details, or the design of God's word. Such arrogance is inexcusable before a jealous and righteous God. The interpreter who would faithfully deliver a message to the brotherhood of Christ and to those who are aliens to God's word must do so with all diligence, integrity and fervor. He must seek to please no man but seek favor with God alone as he approaches the Bible with trembling and an unblemished expectancy to know God's revelation to man. When the Bible speaks plainly, so ought we; when the Bible is silent, we should withhold our words; and when the Bible is unclear, we ought not to confabulate.

Essential Doctrine

A second principle for unity is to define the essential doctrines. This is much easier said than done. Nothing requires more discipline and wisdom than establishing the essentials of the faith. Among the masses of our denominational world, this would appear quite easy since virtually every church has a statement of "what we believe." Turn to any local church's statement of faith, or to the Apostles' Creed, or to some other compilation of words defining tests of fellowship, and you may find ninety-eight percent harmony among them—but the two percent is what divides!

While all such creeds are cognitive fabrications of uninspired men, the best of them do draw heavily upon the fundamental essentials of the Christian faith as set forth in Scripture. The great dilemma for anyone formulating a statement of faith is what to include as essential and what to leave out. Consequently, any official statement of belief, however noble may be the intent of its authors, is necessarily a denominational trap. A creed demands that we pick and choose, and therein lies bias. A statement of faith may ever so subtly and unwittingly introduce a prejudice or partiality that may not be shared by all.

How then shall we declare what are the bare essentials, the true test of fellowship between brothers and sisters in Christ?

This question is not easily answered, and maybe it should not be answered. Does the Bible offer any clear distinctions as to what is essential? No. The Bible cannot be "parted out." It is a whole and must be accepted in its entirety. The apostle Paul instructed the Corinthians to "imitate me, just as I also imitate Christ," and he praised them because they did faithfully "keep the traditions, just as I delivered them to you" (1 Cor. 11:1-2). He also commanded the Thessalonian Christians to "stand fast and hold the traditions which you were taught, whether by word or our epistle" (2 Thess. 2:15), and to "withdraw from every brother who walks disorderly and not according to the tradition which he received from us" (2 Thess. 3:6).

Jesus commissioned His followers to make disciples by baptizing them and "teaching them to observe all that I commanded you" (Matt. 28:20), not just some of the things He commanded us. He made no distinction between any of the principles He taught them. He had no prioritized list. He did not say, "Here, focus on these." Jesus did not compartmentalize, categorize, catalogue, prioritize, outline, or otherwise distinguish between any set of principles that He taught His disciples; and neither should we. He gave no bare minimum essentials. Jesus declared that *all* was to be taught; nothing was declared optional or unessential with regard to holy living.

The formula of a creed of any kind may derive from biblical principles, but it screens and selects certain principles over others, and for this we have no biblical precedent. A creed essentially declares: "This is what we hold to be important. This is what we expect you to believe if you want to be a part of our fellowship." The establishment of a statement of faith may originate from a sincere and good intent of the heart, but all creeds are intrinsically divisive by their very nature. The Bible alone must be our creed. The Bible not only contains the essentials of the faith, it is, in its entirety, the declaration of our faith.

This is not to say that that the Bible does not place a greater emphasis on certain doctrines than on others, or that no chronology of teaching exists. In all his missionary journeys, Paul's emphasis was the crucified and resurrected Christ as the only One who could save. He placed first things first, as it should be.

The writer of Hebrews taught that the "elementary principles of the oracles of God" (Heb. 5:12) were the milk needed by babes in faith, "but solid food is for the mature" (Heb. 5:14). Unfortunately, most professing Christians never move on to maturity, remaining spiritual infants their entire lives. Much of the deeper teachings of the Bible cannot even be taught or understood because of willful spiritual immaturity that the Hebrews writer calls "dullness of hearing" (Heb. 5:12). Such spiritual dwarfs will choke on solid soul-nourishing food just as infants choke if given meat and potatoes. If Christians cannot digest the solid food of the Bible, they will forever be stunted in their spiritual growth. An unholy failure to thrive renders the weak Christian susceptible to deception and to apostasy, thereby leading to a further division of Christ's body.

Obedience to the Faith

This leads to a third tenet necessary for oneness in God's family. If the Bible is our doctrine, then obedience to all the Bible's teachings is required for unity. Unity is a natural consequence of obedience to our true faith. Selective obedience confuses and divides. How sad that this obedience is not taught at conversion; worse yet, the evangelist himself often ignores it.

The making of a disciple for Jesus begins with a knowledge and acceptance of the death, burial and resurrection of Christ. The starting point for all Christians is the message of the cross. It is Jesus Christ, and Him crucified that allows for the gift of eternal life. But Christian conversion must take place according to the way Jesus instructed. Many a preacher and teacher take great pains to purposefully avoid saying what the Bible clearly teaches about conversion because of a refusal to accept the Bible's teaching on the subject as a whole.

Because of this elective ambiguity, we now have popularized in American Christianity the non-biblical teaching that a would-be convert need only "ask Jesus into one's heart." The desired outcome of many modern evangelistic meetings is to lead people to make "a decision" for Christ, suggesting a one-time act consummated perhaps by praying "the sinner's prayer" which has become so popular.

Nowhere in Scripture is this taught or exemplified. Such immature teaching requires a selective ignoring of what the Bible actually commands, and it is taught explicitly to keep the inept evangelist within his denominational comfort zone. This is nothing less than a form of heresy that only serves to confuse the naïve seeker who reads a different account on the sacred pages of holy writ. The acceptance of Christ as Savior is not merely a mental assent of facts to be believed; it is a starting point for a life of sacrificial obedience to the gospel message.

Satan believes in God. He knows that Jesus is the Christ. This is mere mental assent, not conversion. The apostle Paul makes this point very clear in his great exposition of the gospel in the book of Romans. He openly declares that we received the grace offered through Jesus Christ "for obedience to the faith among all nations" (Rom. 1:5). This obedience of faith encompasses all the teachings of the Bible. Nothing but the blood of Jesus can wash away my sins, but Jesus's gift of eternal life, like any other gift, must be accepted. Let not the preacher and teacher, the evangelist and expositor, liquefy the solid teaching of Scripture that "He became the author of eternal salvation to all who obey Him" (Heb. 5:9). Conversion without obedience is no conversion at all. As James, the half-brother of Jesus tells us: "Show me your faith without your works, and I will show you my faith by my works" (Jas. 2:18). Obedience to the faith means doing things God's way.

Genuine Humility

As we contend for the true faith, some of us may declare ourselves spiritual warriors, defenders of the faith, and advocates of all righteousness. We charge forward to prove ourselves worthy of our calling. We put on the armor of God and seek to live out our faith in bold radiance. We seek to be strong in the Lord, to take up the good fight, and to challenge all who would disagree with us. But have you noticed how much of the fighting is among *us*, the Christians? How easily we forget that "we do not wrestle against flesh and blood, but against principalities, against powers, against the rulers of the darkness of this age, against spiritual hosts of wickedness in the heavenly places" (Eph. 6:12).

The enemy within our churches does certainly exist, but oftentimes we wrongly vilify our fellow disciples in Christ because we do not all think exactly alike. All who seek to please our Lord walk a fine line between being commanded to think alike in the sense of having the mind of Christ (1 Cor. 2:16) while also allowing for liberty in Christ with regard to burdens of conscience, as discussed in Romans chapter fourteen. How do we pull this off? It seems tricky.

A genuine sincerity of heart is needed to search out the deep truths of Scripture, and humility of mind is needed to rightly convey those truths. Although perfect scholarship in Bible interpretation should be our utmost goal, defective scholarship seems to be the norm. Sincerity and zeal are good, but without knowledge they can be a destructive force in the brotherhood. A genuine humility of spirit is essential to bringing us together as a unified body of Christ. If we would dare to be honest, we all cherish some pet doctrines that may not align with the Bible's intended message. We are all stronger in some areas of Bible knowledge than others. We are both the stronger and the weaker brother in various realms of our spiritual walk. But in my own experience among those who profess a devout faith, those who speak the loudest often walk the weakest.

Humility of heart goes a long way in sweetening Christian fellowship and in helping fellow Christians to graciously accept an error in their understanding of Scripture or in living aright. Vehemence in expounding truth must be tempered with gentleness and patience. Just as truth should never be compromised, neither must it be shoved down a dissenter's gullet. Fighting over doctrine has never yielded any bountiful fruit among the brotherhood of believers. A humble personal quest for truth in Scripture is much more fruitful than a flagrant proclamation of pet (and sometimes petty) dogma. We must put away the pious veneer and infuse some genuine humility when searching out and proclaiming Bible truths. We should study hard, pray often, and speak softly. Only then shall cohesion in the group be more likely to prevail in the presence of truth.

This humility also applies to reaching those outside of the church. In every age, the greatest turnoff to the unbeliever is the incivility Christians display to the world in a telling show of hypocrisy. History has taught us that more souls have been won for Christ through sincere kindness than through browbeating with Scripture. Let us also remember that the greatest testimony to the world of the power of Christ in us is our demonstration of love toward one another and toward those outside of the faith. We are told throughout the Bible in so many ways and so many times that love is the greatest force for good in the world. This love is one of unconditional regard and declares that, "You are just as important as me." Such love is hard to turn down, and it certainly does not go unnoticed. Combined with truth and gentleness, love wins souls. If you commit to proclaim the gospel in humility and truth, you will certainly bear good fruit in growing the church.

The Quintessential Unifier

If there be any one principle that must be followed to achieve unity in the church on any Bible teaching, it would be wrapped up in one very simple question: What does the Bible say? Whether speaking of salvation, creation, holy living, group fellowship, evangelism, generosity, parenting, prayer, or any other Christian teaching—ask the question! What does the Bible say? Better yet, what does the Bible really say?

This question honors God. And if we seek to answer it with a blank slate openness to truth, with the simplicity of a child, and with all humility and integrity of heart, then the answer shall likely be found. A Berean spirit is a unifying spirit. The Bereans "received the word with all readiness" (Acts 17:11), that is, with a blank-slate form of open-mindedness. They didn't refute, contradict, or argue. Nor did they ignore, downgrade, nullify, or reject the teachings of Paul and Silas. They listened. Then afterwards, they opened the book (or scrolls) to see exactly what the Scriptures had to say about what was being preached to them, to determine if what Paul and Silas claimed actually aligned with the already written words of the Old Testament that were in their possession. What a beautiful example to follow.

Although we now have a completed record of God's full revelation of Himself for almost 2000 years, most Christians do not realize that some of the beliefs popularized in twenty-first century American Christianity were not always prominent or accepted. Since the first century, many new teachings and nuances of faith have been preached, many of which were formerly very unpopular among Christians. Some present-day beliefs are brazenly wrong, being biblically unfounded. Distortions and misunderstandings of sacred teachings abound, and many of these are blindly accepted solely because they are preached from a pulpit and therefore assumed legitimate. Such spiritual indolence has been the cause of many fissures in the universal church. We must not be lazy and undiscerning listeners when we hear sermonizing of "Christianity with a twist." Many trusted spiritual leaders are all too willing to advance an unholy agenda because they love money and power more than the things of God. We ought always to be on guard, to listen with eagerness, and to ask ourselves, is this really what the Bible tells us? **What does *the Bible* say?** This is the paramount question that leads to a unified and solid church.

Chapter 12
A Call for Unity without Compromise

The knitting together of all who follow Christ must forever be pursued through the filters of love and truth; compromising no Scripture, while maintaining a spirit of true humility and leaving the final judgment of our hearts to the Author of all love and truth. In our proclamation of God to both the Christian disciple and the unconverted masses, we must never forget who makes the rules. Jesus the Warrior-King is He. And this Jesus, who declares to us His ultimate victory over all the sinister forces of evil, reminds us at the end of his revelation that we shall be held strictly accountable for our handling of Scripture. This warning is grave and has eternal consequences. Woe to the deceiver and to the false proclaimer!

The apostle John warns, "If anyone adds to these things, God will add to him the plagues that are written in this book; and if anyone takes away from the words of the book of this prophecy, God shall take away his part from the Book of Life, from the holy city, and from the things which are written in this book" (Rev. 22:18-19).

No platitudes or slovenly disregard will serve as an excuse for the willful or careless error of misrepresenting God's message.

This warning is not one to be trifled with. If we opt to not change the status quo of our denominational stereotypes for the sake of retaining power, financial gain, comfortable complacency, or the favor of so-called Christian elites, then we risk the same condemnation as the Pharisees who preferred the perks of their self-serving traditions to the truth of God's word. We ought to muster the courage to look into the mirror and ask God to expose our own shades of iniquity that cover our hearts. Better to humbly repent of any hint of calloused apostasy now than to be told in the hereafter, "I never knew you; depart from Me, you who practice lawlessness" (Matt. 7:23).

This response from Jesus was not directed toward those lacking a form of religion, as they protested, "Lord, Lord, have we not prophesied in Your name, cast out demons in Your name, and done many wonders in Your name?" (Matt. 7:22). Despite all the glitter and glam, Jesus declared them to be strangers to Him. Can you imagine hearing those words from our Lord on the Day of Judgment? We would do well to heed the words of James who tells us to "receive with meekness the implanted word, which is able to save our souls" (James 1:21). We are forewarned in John's gospel that we are given no valid license to change the rules, to call the shots when it comes to being a Christian. Jesus sternly admonished those who would challenge the Lord's way of doing things. "Most assuredly I say to you, he who does not enter the sheepfold by the door, but climbs up some other way, the same is a thief and a robber" (John 10:1). Jesus then declares Himself figuratively to be that door. The message is clear. We must follow the teachings of Christ and of Him alone. Any new gospel or spurious teaching derives from a false shepherd who will lead us through the wrong door—the door of condemnation.

But what comfort we have in the words of Isaiah 55:6-7, urging us: "Seek the Lord while He may be found, call upon Him while He is near. Let the wicked forsake his way, and the unrighteous man his thoughts; and let him return to the Lord, and He will have mercy on him; and to our God, for He will abundantly pardon." If we desire to return to the Lord, then we must return to the Scriptures.

A one-mind, one-body church is completely dependent upon the power of God to overcome four major obstacles to unity, all without compromise of any Bible teaching. First, the power to fully understand all things in Scripture is simply beyond our mental capability. Second, we shall forever struggle with our own sinful nature of pride and selfishness in this earthly body. Third, deep in our hearts are contained seeds of doubt, insecurity, and a strong desire to belong. And fourth, we must concede that God has chosen not to disclose to us all things.

We can only speculate through composition of our vivid imagination, for example, the details of how Jesus shall return again. We are given a few broad strokes of the brush, but no specific details about His return are painted for us. Yet as we eagerly await His return, we understandably long to know the particulars. Many church leaders are all too ready to capitalize on this desire, and they may offer colorful renditions of such biblical uncertainties, all for the sake of selfish gain. How do we ever accept the fact that what we haven't yet been given, we have no need to know? We certainly are given all the instructions we need for our salvation and for living a righteous life in Christ. Such teachings should be our chief focus rather than spending exorbitant amounts of time and energy on speculative and controversial things. "The secret things belong to the Lord our God, but those things which are revealed belongs to us and to our children forever, that we may do all the words of this law" (Deut. 29:29). The doing of these revealed words confirms in us the faith that we proclaim. This should be our primary focus.

Of course, history and the Bible teach that a unified church will only exist in the realm of heaven following Christ's return. But if each of us strives to be a "body-builder" by sharpening our interpretive skills and committing to not propagate false and questionable teachings, unity among believers will prevail to a significantly greater degree than what we now see.

As always has been, now is the time to unify and reach out to the world. The history of mankind shall surely have its conclusion, and the clock is ticking on our temporal world. Whereas nobody knows the exact time of Christ's return for the great Judgment of the world, the time is nearer now than yesterday. Perhaps we can do more to lead others to the life-changing truths of Scripture than we have done before. Nobody who embraces a counterfeit Christianity can avail any lasting good. People need the real Christ. Sinners must hear the real truth in Scripture. Christians must obey this truth without compromise, forever striving toward maturity by being solidly rooted in the word of God so we do not fall away during the time of temptation. As Christ's disciples, we must taste "the good word of God and the powers of the age to come" (Heb. 6:5) and hold fast those words with all tenacity. In doing so, we build the church, and we receive a blessing now and for eternity. Let us take up "the sword of the Spirit, which is the word of God" (Eph. 6:17), and let us sharpen it and use it in battle to slay not one another, but the real enemy of God.

Throughout this book, I have shed a dark light on sectarianism, and I make no apologies for it. The stronger one's denominational affiliation, the weaker is one's loyalty to the unity of all believers for which Jesus prayed. Our first duty is to uphold as our banner the integrity of the entirety of God's word. To do otherwise is to engage in rebellion against God. "But the person who does anything presumptuously, whether he is native-born or a stranger, that one brings reproach on the Lord, and he shall be cut off from among his people. Because he has despised the word of the Lord... his guilt shall be upon him" (Num. 15:30-31).

Better that our words be few and accurate than many and untrue. Let us be called people of the Book rather than people of the balk. May we precisely and diligently learn God's word and proclaim it for the sake of unifying and gathering all who would respond to those words. Jesus warned, "He who is not with Me is against Me, and he who does not gather with Me scatters abroad" (Matt. 12:30). In other words, if we are not actively doing things God's way, then we are working against Him. Any twisting of the Scriptures is deviant and ungodly behavior. People generally do not tolerate any challenge to their belief system for all the reasons previously mentioned, but we must realize that our happiness, joy and emotional stability are always compromised by any falsehood.

In recent years, we have actually observed a curious turn in the right direction, as many denominational churches are dropping their sectarian titles. An article in the Star Tribune mentions that Trinity Baptist Church in Maplewood renamed itself "LifePoint." "Maple Grove Evangelical Free Church just converted to 'The Grove," and First Lutheran Church in White Bear Lake is now "Community of Grace."[1] It seems their motive is to avoid the sectarian label in the hope of attracting younger people who may otherwise suspiciously spurn a certain partisan absolute.

Given that church attendance in the new millennial age is dwindling, this may be simply a strategic maneuver. The younger population is profoundly noncommittal, opposed to any type of obliged conformity, and distanced from group interaction because of their obsession with electronics and social media. Dropping denominational labels and rebranding with trendy names may open the door to the ranks of this new mindset. If their goal is evangelistic outreach, then more power to them. This is good. Even if their motive is wrong, the move is a good one. Rebranding does not necessarily mean restructuring, but it does remove the denominational title that intrinsically divides the Christian body.

However, if churches are not also moving toward a more biblically supported gathering of Christians, their ploy shall be in vain. As James Emery White opines "The trend I see is oriented to jump-starting a dead battery."[2] If this church trend is designed to dilute the gospel message in favor of an "all are welcome" and "anything goes" design, then the church may indeed grow in numbers, but wane proportionally in spiritual force. God has never placed a value on salesmanship, but He greatly regards faithfulness and obedience.

Reflections on A Unified Christian Church

The writing of any book on such a serious and profound topic as Christian unity is sure to raise some emotional dander. Even a book written for the sake of harmony and unity may unintentionally be divisive. Asking for us all to critically analyze and question our most cherished spiritual beliefs is intimidating and unnerving. It strikes us at the very core of our beings.

Much like an undiagnosed cancer, some would prefer to remain ignorant despite the importance of knowing something is wrong. They would rather forego the CT scan that would diagnose the malignancy in hope of a cure, not realizing that without remedy, their next appointment will be with the mortuary .

Any challenge to our deepest spiritual beliefs is threatening, and our natural first impulse is always to recoil from any threat of emotional pain. A fight or flight response is triggered. Sometimes truth is painful. Reading this book has undoubtedly caused some gritting of teeth, and some readers may even look upon this author with sheer contempt. I most sincerely apologize for any offense. but I do not apologize for my position.

We all have spiritual wounds, and none of us have full spiritual clarity or perfect discernment. Like you the reader, I have struggled in my search for biblical truth. I too long to be accepted, and I tend to flinch at any challenge to my faith. Like you, I can only cry mercy at the feet of a loving and forgiving God when my journey here ends. And mercy we shall receive if we follow God's plan for the salvation of our souls. But we also now have the burden of accountability to be faithful to Christ alone, to the righteous teachings of Scripture alone, without bias, distortion, or compromise. I would hope that any transgression of my own words or deeds is a product of personal ignorance rather than a mistake of the heart. I can assert with a clear conscience that my impetus for penning this tome is nothing less than a plea for the unity that Jesus Himself prayed for to our Father, "that the world may believe."

We have strayed far and wide as a brotherhood of Christian believers. We live in a time in America when Christians are becoming ever weaker in Bible doctrine, precisely as Christian values are being attacked from every angle. If we as a Christian nation fall from God's grace through our failure to be united as Jesus petitioned His Father, then we shall certainly suffer all the wrathful consequences of man's lust for power, wealth, and depravity.

A counterfeit Christianity will never survive the onslaught of evil we now see frothing on the horizon. Throughout history, God has called forth faithful messengers to summon His people back to the pure and basic truths of His word. Woe to those who do not harken to His call. The question before each of us is, will we choose to be a voice for God's agenda or for our own? If we unite as Christians who love and obey the Book, we stand strong to thwart all that is evil in our world. Elsewise, we allow evil to have its way.

God has chosen you and me to be a beacon of His light and truth in this sin-darkened world. We must remember that Jesus used some of the lowliest of characters to accomplish His highest purpose, and He did so with great success. How comforting to know that God's all-loving, all-powerful design is sure to be fulfilled in every minute detail, despite despicable me, and maybe you. I simply pray that you and I will allow Christ to be the Lord of our lives over all manmade institutions, decrees, and traditions. I hope that He might acknowledge me among the least of His many faithful ambassadors who preached His word with integrity, knowing that I did my best to be a tiny instrument of the answer to His prayer for oneness. And I pray that you will join me in that quest. Amen.

Endnotes

[1] Jean Hopfensperger, "What's in a name? Churches trade old names for new, younger members," *Star Tribune*, April 15, 2017, <startribune.com>, accessed on August 24, 2019.

[2] James Emery White, "Is Renaming a Church Going to Change Anything?," 2013, <christianity.com>, accessed on August 24, 2019.

Bibliography

Alexander, David, and Patricia Alexander, eds., *Eerdmans' Handbook to the Bible*, Eerdmans, Grand Rapids, 1973.

Anthony, Edward, *The Final Request of Jesus is Complete Christian Unity*, Southern Oaks Publishing, southernoakspublishing@hotmail.com, 2013.

"Back to the Basics," AllAtHisFeet@cs.com, Indianapolis, 2008.

Barna, George, *Evangelism That Works*, Regal Books, Ventura, CA, 1995.

Billheimer, Paul E., *Love Covers: A Viable Platform for Christian Unity*, Christian Literature Crusade, Fort Washington, PA, 1981.

Bilheimer, Robert S., *The Quest for Christian Unity*, Haddam House, New York, 1952.

Braaten, Carl E., and Robert W. Jenson, eds., *In One Body Through the Cross*, Eerdmans, Grand Rapids, 2003.

Brand, Paul, and Philip Yancey, *Fearfully & Wonderfully Made*, Zondervan, Grand Rapids, 1980.

Bromiley, Geoffrey W., ed., *The International Standard Bible Encyclopedia*, Eerdmans, Grand Rapids, 1988.

Bruce, Frederick F., *The Canon of Scripture*, InterVarsity Press, Downers Grove, 1988.

— — — , *The Hard Sayings of Jesus*, InterVarsity Press, Downers Grove, 1983.

Bullinger, E. W., *Figures of Speech Used in the Bible*, Baker Book House, Grand Rapids, 1968.

Callen, Barry L., and James B. North, *Coming Together in Christ*, College Press, Joplin, 1997.

Cottrell, Jack, *Baptism*, College Press, Joplin, 1989.

— — — , *Gender Roles & the Bible*, College Press, Joplin, 1994.

— — — , *The Holy Spirit*, College Press, Joplin, 2006.

Crabb, Larry, *Real Church*, Thomas Nelson, Nashville, 2009.

Dawson, Samuel G., *Fellowship with God and His People*, 2nd ed., SGD Press, Bowie, TX, 2004.

Earle, Ralph, *Word Meanings in the New Testament*, Baker Book House, Grand Rapids, 1986.

FaLardeau, Ernest, *That All May Be One*, Paulist Press, New York, 2000.

Gower, Ralph, *The New Manners and Customs of Bible Times*, Moody Press, Chicago, 1987.

Johnson, David, and Jeff VanVonderen, *The Subtle Power of Spiritual Abuse*, Bethany House Publishers, Minneapolis, 1991.

Ketcherside, W. Carl, *The Twisted Scriptures*, Mission Messenger, Saint Louis, 1965.

Kinnaman, David, and Gabe Lyons, *Unchristian*, Baker Books, Grand Rapids, 2007.

Kittel, Gerhard, and Gerhard Friedrich, *Theological Dictionary of the New Testament*, Abridged in one volume by Geoffrey W. Bromiley, Eerdmans, Grand Rapids, 1985.

Kurosaki, Kokichi, *Let's Return to Christian Unity*, Christian Books, Auburn, ME, 1991.

Lloyd-Jones, Martyn D., *The Basis of Christian Unity*, The Banner of Truth Trust, Carlisle, PA, 2003.

———, *Christian Unity*, Baker, Grand Rapids, 1980.

Maier, Gerhard, *Biblical Hermeneutics*, Crossway Books, Wheaton, 1994.

MacArthur, John, ed., *Fool's Gold?*, Crossway Books, Wheaton, 2005.

———, *The Master's Plan for the Church*, Moody Press, Chicago, 1991.

Macquarrie, John, *Principles of Christian Theology*, 2nd ed., Charles Scribner's Sons, New York, 1977.

McManus, Erwin R., *An Unstoppable Force*, Group, Loveland, CO, 2001.

Mead, Frank S., et al., eds., *Handbook of Denominations in the United States*, 12th ed., Abingdon Press, Nashville, 2005.

Meninger, Karl, *Whatever Became of Sin?*, Hawthorn Books, New York, 1973.

Mickelsen, A. Berkeley, *Interpreting the Bible*, Eerdmans, Grand Rapids, 1974.

Mullin, Robert B., and Russell E. Richey, *Reimagining Denominationalism*, Oxford University Press, New York, 1994.

Murch, James D., *Christians Only*, Standard Publishing, Cincinnati, 1962.

North, James B., *Union in Truth*, Standard Publishing, Cincinnati, 1994.

Olbricht, Thomas H., and Hans Rollmann, eds., *The Quest for Christian Unity, Peace, and Purity in Thomas Campbell's Declaration and Address*, Scarecrow Press, Landham, MD, 2000.

Olson, Roger E., *The Mosaic of Christian Belief*, InterVarsity Press, Downers Grove, 2002.

Outler, Albert C., *The Christian Tradition and the Unity We Seek*, Oxford University, New York, 1957.

Pink, Arthur W., *Interpretation of the Scripture*, Baker, Grand Rapids, 1972.

Ramm, Bernard, *Protestant Biblical Interpretation*, 3rd ed., Baker Book House, Grand Rapids, 1970.

Richards, Lawrence O., *A New Face for the Church*, Zondervan, Grand Rapids, 1970.

Riddlebarger, Kim, *The Man of Sin*, Baker, Grand Rapids, 2006.

Riley-Smith, Jonathan, ed., *The Oxford Illustrated History of the Crusades*, Oxford University Press, Oxford, 1995.

Rinehart, Stacey, and Paula Rinehart, *Living in Light of Eternity*, NavPress, Colorado Springs, 1986.

Robinson, Haddon W., *Biblical Preaching*, Baker, Grand Rapids, 1980.

Roose, Kevin, *The Unlikely Disciple*, Grand Central Publishing, New York, 2009.

Ryken, Leland, *How to Read the Bible as Literature*, Zondervan, Grand Rapids, 1984.

Schaeffer, Francis A., *The Mark of the Christian*, InterVarsity Press, Downers Grove, 1970.

Shelley, Marshall, *Well-Intentioned Dragons*, Word Publishing, Dallas, 1985.

Sire, James W., *Scripture Twisting*, InterVarsity Press, Downers Grove, 1980.

Slipper, Callan, *Five Steps to Living Christian Unity*, New City Press, Hyde Park, NY, 2013.

Smith, Joseph, *Joseph Smith Tells His Own Story*, pamphlet published by the Church of Jesus Christ of Latter-day Saints.

Strauch, Alexander, *Biblical Eldership*, Lewis and Roth Publishers, Littleton, CO, 1995.

Unger, Merrill F., *Unger's Bible Dictionary*, Moody Press, Chicago, 1957.

About the Author

Steven A. LaTulippe, MD, is a practicing family physician, a retired United States Air Force officer and aviator, an ordained minister, and a diligent student of God's word. He attended Boise Bible College and Cincinnati Bible Seminary, and has always delighted in the study of sound interpretation of Scripture. His yearning to bring Christians together as a force for good in the world arises from visiting many churches across the nation and globe, always seeing the unlimited potential of those who faithfully work to serve our mighty Lord, Jesus Christ.

9 781630 501471